EGYPT

EGYPT

The Moment of Change

Edited by

Rabab El-Mahdi & Philip Marfleet

Zed Books

LONDON & NEW YORK

Egypt: The Moment of Change was first published in 2009 by
Zed Books Ltd, 7 Cynthia Street, London N1 9JF, UK and
Room 400, 175 Fifth Avenue, New York, NY 10010, USA

www.zedbooks.co.uk

Editorial Copyright © Rabab El-Mahdi and Philip Marfleet 2009
Copyright in this collection © Zed Books 2009

The rights of Rabab El-Mahdi and Philip Marfleet to be identified
as the authors of this work have been asserted by them in
accordance with the Copyright, Designs and Patents Act, 1988

FSC
Mixed Sources
Product group from well-managed
forests and other controlled sources
Cert no. SGS-COC-2953
www.fsc.org
© 1996 Forest Stewardship Council

Designed and typeset in Monotype Janson
by illuminati, Grosmont, www.illuminatibooks.co.uk
Cover designed by Lucy Morton @ illuminati
Index by Philip Marfleet
Cover photograph © Joan Bellver
Printed and bound in Great Britain by
CPI Antony Rowe, Chippenham and Eastbourne

Distributed in the USA exclusively by Palgrave Macmillan, a division
of St Martin's Press, LLC, 175 Fifth Avenue, New York, NY 10010, USA

A catalogue record for this book is available from the British Library
Library of Congress Cataloging in Publication Data available

ISBN 978 1 84813 020 3 Hb
ISBN 978 1 84813 021 0 Pb
ISBN 978 1 84813 504 8 Eb

Contents

Glossary

Terms and names in Arabic

awqaf religious endowments (sing. *waqf*)

aysh bread; *aysh baladi* (made with wholewheat flour); *asysh shami* (made with white flour)

feddan measurement of land area: 0.42 hectare, or 1.038 acres

fellah peasant, farmer (pl. *fellahin*)

fuul fava beans

gallabeyya loose-fitting male/female garment

halat al-tawari' state of emergency

hijab headscarf for women

iftar meal that breaks Ramadan fast after sunset

infitah opening; *al-infitah al-iqtisadi* – economic opening

intifada uprising, upheaval

jihad striving, exertion, fight, war

manabir pulpits (sing. *minbar*)

niqab cloth covering the face

al-nizam the system

pasha senior rank in the Ottoman political system; used in Egypt until 1952

sharia laws of Islam

shura consultation; also the name of the upper house of the Egyptian parliament

State agencies, political parties and movements

Amn al-Markazi   Central Security Force – CSF
Gama'at Islamiyya   Islamic Groups (variously called Gama'a Islamiya, al-Jamaat al-Islamiya, al-Gama'a al-Islamiyya)
al-Harakat al-Tag'eer   Movements for Change
al-Hay'aat al-Tahrir   Liberation Agency
Hamla Sha'biya min Agl al-Tag'eer   Popular Campaign for Change
al-Hizb al-Watani al-Dimuqrati   National Democratic Party (NDP)
al-Ikhwan al-Muslimin   Muslim Brotherhood
al-Ittihad al-Ishtiraqi   Socialist Union
al-Ittihad al-Qawmi   National Union
Jihaz Amn al-Dawla   State Security Service
Jihaz al-Amn al-Qawmi   National Security Service
Kifaya   Enough! Slogan of the Egyptian Movement for Change and name by which it is usually known
Majlis al-Shaab   People's Assembly (lower house of parliament)
Majlis al-Shura   Shura Council (upper house of parliament)
Mabaheth Amn al-Dawla   General Directorate of State Security Investigations
al-Mukhabarat al-Aama   General Intelligence and Security Service
al-Mukhabarat al-Harbeya   Military Intelligence Service
Nadi al-Quda   Judges' Club
al-Tagammu'   National Progressive Unionist Party
Wafd   'Delegation' Party

Abbreviations and acronyms

ANHRI   Arabic Network for Human Rights Information
ASU   Arab Socialist Union
EAAT   Egyptian Association Against Torture
EOHR   Egyptian Organisation for Human Rights
ERSAP   Economic Reform and Structural Adjustment Programme
ETUF   *al-Ittihad al-'Amm li-Niqabat 'Ummal Misr,* Egyptian Trade Union Federation (also known as EFTU)
IFI   international financial institution
LCHR   Land Center for Human Rights
NDP   National Democratic Party
NEPAD   New Partnership for Africa's Development
UNHCR   Office of the United Nations High Commissioner for Refugees

Preface and acknowledgements

This book examines economy, politics and society at a key moment in modern Egyptian history. But its point of departure is not the economy or political system as such; rather, it is the active engagement of Egyptians attempting urgently to bring change in their own lives and as part of projects for wider social transformation.

In the 1970s Egypt became a laboratory for economic changes later imposed worldwide as part of the neoliberal agenda for development. The outcome has been striking, providing important long-term evidence of how 'marketisation' affects society at large. While a minority of Egyptians have accumulated unprecedented wealth, the mass of people experience greater poverty and insecurity; at the same time they are victims of a suffocating autocracy. Like many states of the Global South, Egypt is ruled by a regime committed both to the 'free' market and to the denial of political reform. It is in this context that scores of millions of Egyptians struggle to meet basic needs and to secure fundamental rights.

There is a dearth of information and analysis on Egypt for the general reader. This book attempts to tackle the deficit; at the same time it seeks to bring together materials of interest to academics, researchers, students and others concerned directly with Egypt and the Middle East, and with issues of change in the Global South. It draws upon a wealth of material usually available only in specialist publications, upon Arabic-language sources, and – selectively – upon data and analysis from the Egyptian media, notably from the independent press and the e-networks. It does not attempt a comprehensive review of contemporary society: we do not offer a detailed economic history of modern Egypt, nor of dominant institutions of the Egyptian state. And we are conscious that matters of cultural change, gender, law, minority rights and personal status require to be addressed much more fully. We hope nonetheless that this collaboration stimulates discussion on questions which are now of pressing importance.

So many people were inspiring and supportive during the process of producing this book: most importantly the contributors, without whom we would not have been able to write an acknowledgement. All of them are busy and yet have found the time and enthusiasm to share their insights with us. Special thanks are due to our editor Tamsine O'Riordan of Zed Books.

For me this book was inspired by the unyielding persistence of Egyptian women and men trying to make the world a better place. Shahenda Maqlad and the late Wedad Metri have been iconic inspirations; Aida and Kemal, my appreciation for what you do is beyond words. The friendship of Maha Abdel Rahman and so many interesting discussions have been of immense help. Finally, my family – Mom, Dad, Mostafa and Sameh – have kept me going well before this book and throughout the process. Their insurmountable support through bad times I will always cherish.

Rabab El-Mahdi

A host of people have inspired us and assisted us: our sincere thanks and assurances that the errors and omissions remain our own. Special thanks to Tamsine O'Riordan, our editor at Zed Books, who has been remarkably patient and supportive – and to Fran Cetti, for her special expertise in bibliographical matters. I would like to acknowledge in particular the patience and forbearance of my partner Lynne Hubbard, of Harry Hubbard and of Ellie Marfleet (again!), and the continuing support of my father Gerry Marfleet, who inspired me to think about Egypt, and much more. Thanks to former and current colleagues at the University of East London (UEL) especially Denis Cattell, Alan

O'Shea, Gavin Poynter and Haim Bresheeth, who facilitated many extended visits to Cairo. Thanks also to John Nassari, Sue Cohen and Diane Ball, and to the students and staff of International Development and of Refugee Studies at UEL, with whom I've been able to enjoy so many stimulating visits to the city.

Finally, my thanks and wishes to co-editor Rabab El-Mahdi, and to Enid Hill, Khalid Fahmy, Tareq Ismael, Aida Seif El-Dawla, Yahya Fikri, Kemal Khalil, Sameh Naguib, Wael Khalil, Wael Gamal, Hossam el-Hamalawy, John Rose, Anne Alexander and many other friends who, for the present, I cannot name.

Philip Marfleet

This book is dedicated to Yusuf Darwish (1910–2006)
and to Nabil al-Hilali (1928–2006) –
revolutionaries, activists, intellectuals and fighters
to the very end

Introduction

Rabab El-Mahdi & Philip Marfleet

Egypt attracts intense interest. Documentaries, feature films, books and magazines celebrate Egypt – but not the Egypt of today. It is Egypt of the pharaohs that draws screen directors and the authors of guides, special supplements and historical novels. Even among academic specialists there are few analyses of the range of contemporary issues. This book attempts to fill some of the gaps, addressing questions about economy, politics and society at a crucial moment in the history of the most populous and most influential country in the Arab world.

By 2009 Husni Mubarak had been president of Egypt continuously for twenty-eight years: only seven other heads of state had held power for longer.[1] Even under a veneer of party pluralism, systemic political changes have been blocked through rigged elections which have maintained Mubarak's National Democratic Party (NDP) rule for more than three decades. His authoritarian regime has supervised a huge increase in social inequality: a minority has accumulated unprecedented wealth while more and more people live at the margin of survival. The privileged few are protected by an armed force of unprecedented size operating under an official State of Emergency in force since 1981. Public protest is forbidden by law and in most cases severely punished by police and security agencies which maintain a regime of systematic abuse. Torture has become routine: the Egyptian Association Against Torture believes that such abuse is part of a strategy – 'to terrorize individuals and to ensure complete submission of the people'.[2]

Most Egyptians struggle to meet basic needs. Access to essential foods involves daily difficulties: across the country, queues form at bakeries at which supplies of bread are often unreliable. Over a few weeks in 2008, fifteen people died in fights among people competing for *aysh baladi* – the loaves which are vital for survival of the mass of Egyptians (Samaan 2008). Millions also struggle for access to drinking water: in 2007 and 2008 there were demonstrations across towns of the Nile Delta in what the local press called a 'Revolution of the Thirsty'. Large numbers of people are on the move from rural areas, while in the cities unemployment has risen sharply. The global crisis which began in 2008 has affected the economy profoundly, with huge falls in foreign investment, tourism, remittances and other key sources of income, relentlessly increasing pressures upon the poor.

Political activists, independent media, academics, lawyers, judges and (when they can be heard) millions of Egyptians demand change, and since 2000 a series of initiatives for reform has focused on democratisation and basic rights. The regime rejects them – after an initial hesitation it has renewed the practice of assaulting demonstrations and meetings and of imprisoning political activists, peasants, students, journalists and writers. But one constituency, the workers' movement, has proved more difficult to control. Successful strikes in both state and private sectors have encouraged the largest and broadest labour movement for more than fifty years. Can the new movements make a difference, or is Egypt to remain a violent autocracy which punishes even the aspiration for reform? Will rising anger and desperation cause explosions of popular protest like those of the past? How will the regime react? Can it survive? Can Egyptians endure another fifty years without change?

Laboratory for neoliberalism[3]

Developments in Egypt have profound implications for the region and at the global level. In 2007 the World Bank described Egypt as 'the world's top reformer'.[4] It praised government policies said to encourage business, reduce bureaucracy, improve access to credit and facilitate trade. President Mubarak has been lauded as a far-sighted strategist able to overcome internal problems and make his country fit for the global era. The business press in Cairo depicts him as a favourite of international financial institutions and Egypt as 'an IMF poster child' (Mabrouk and El-Bakry 2004). Egypt has been offered as a model of the sort canvassed in the 1970s when Mexico was 'top reformer' and in the 1980s when Argentina was presented as an example to the world. Mexico fell from grace during the debt default of 1982 and Argentina collapsed in ignominy with the crash of 2001, thrusting millions of people into poverty and despair.[5] Will Egypt prove an effective champion of neoliberalism?

In the mid-1970s Mubarak's predecessor, Anwar Sadat, introduced a policy of *infitah* – the 'opening' or 'open door'. Foreign capital entered an economy that for twenty years had been largely closed to the world market; at the same time Egypt's own private capitalists were prompted to renew activities inhibited by earlier nationalisations of industry and by land reform. The policy was encouraged by external experts who soon became familiar figures in Cairo:

> There came... bankers; businessmen and representatives; advisers, experts and consultants with their Samsonite cases and their bulging portfolios and prospectuses. They were going to instruct the Egyptian government how to run its economy on sensible Western lines; they were going to help repair or replace the country's groaning, over-burdened infrastructure; they were going to teach the fellaheen of the Delta how to 'maximise' their grain output, and bring Harvard Business School methods to dark, insanitary Cairo shopfloors. (Hirst and Beeson 1981: 207)

Sadat worked closely with these advisers from the World Bank, the International Monetary Fund (IMF) and the United States Agency for International Development (USAID). In January 1977 his government faced massive protests over IMF-inspired cuts to subsidies of foods and fuel – an 'intifada of bread' against which he mobilised the full force of the army. Egypt was set on the neoliberal path, with all its implications for economic restructuring, public welfare and social order. Its regional role and international standing were also to change radically.

As neoliberal orthodoxy gained momentum worldwide similar formulas were being applied across the Global South, with little regard to the impact on society at large. In Egypt, Mubarak repeatedly warned international financial institutions that more political upheavals were likely and that they threatened the stability of the regime and of the entire region; at the same time he fell into line with their demands (Momani 2005). In 1984, after further cuts to subsidies, there were mass protests in the city of Kafr al-Dawwar and, as in 1977, the army intervened with overwhelming force (Bayat 1993). A pattern had been established whereby the Egyptian state continued to implement neoliberal agendas, notwithstanding the price to be paid by the most vulnerable members of society.

'An increasingly divided nation'

For partisans of capitalist globalisation Egypt is an important example of the progressive character of the neoliberal project. They see its recent history as proof of the inevitability of market advance – what Biersteker (2000: 156) calls the 'apparent "triumph" of neoclassical economic thinking throughout the developing world'. During the 1950s and 1960s President Nasser brought much of the economy under state control, establishing an extensive welfare system and guaranteeing food security. Little of his project remains. By the mid-1990s Mubarak and his officials had become fervent privatisers: Momani (2005: 66) comments that they were so keen on impressing IMF staff with a 'bold and aggressive privatization plan' that they offered to sell 'one [public] company per week'. Electricity, water, sanitation, irrigation, health care, transport, telecommunications and education have all since been opened in varying ways to private enterprise.

When in 2005 stock markets in Cairo and Alexandria joined the International Federation of Stock Exchanges as its first Arab members, Egyptian officials boasted of 'growing confidence by international institutions in capabilities of Egyptian market and economy [*sic*]' and a 'remarkable level of economic performance as a result of reform measures adopted by the government' (Egypt State Information Service 2005). In 2006 Prime Minister Ahmed Nazif asserted that economic reform went 'hand in hand with social development programmes, two sides of the same coin, fostering comprehensive development across society' (El-Din 2006). These assessments are questioned even by friends of the regime. The *Financial Times*, which has long lauded Mubarak's economic policy, points to huge increases in inequality and to growing immiseration, commenting nervously on 'Echoes of a pharaonic past' and 'an increasingly divided nation ... the gulf between the haves and the have-nots' (Burns 2000; *Financial Times*, 2007).

The World Bank (2007a) demonstrates that between 2000 and 2005 the proportion of Egyptians living in 'moderate' poverty (defined as income of less than $2 a day) increased from 16.7 per cent to 19.6 per cent – over 15 million people. Such estimates are conservative – based on the arbitrary index of $2 they exclude tens of millions who live at or just above the official poverty line and who are profoundly affected by increases in the price of food and fuel and/or by problems of supply. In 2006 Handoussa, lead author of a United Nations report on Egypt, suggested that 'The state must be held responsible for failing to effectively integrate the more marginalised sectors of Egyptian society' (Unocha 2006). In 2008, following publication of the UNDP's *Egypt Development Report*, she again noted the link between impoverishment and economic reform, observing that 'the poverty gap' had been growing both in relative and in absolute terms (Nkrumah 2008).

Differences in wealth and patterns of consumption are strikingly clear in a new geography of Egyptian urban life. Since the mid-1990s gated communities have appeared in fast-growing neighbourhoods constructed on Cairo's desert fringe. Part of a global phenomenon (similar enclaves have appeared in a series of states in Africa, Asia and Latin America), they reveal much about the neoliberal model. Constructed on state-owned land offered for sale as part of the reform process, and provided with state-funded infrastructure, they invite the nouveau riche to become part of a 'spectacle of elite distinction' (Denis 2006: 64). In a process that parallels recent de-sequestration[6] of rural land taken under state ownership in the 1950s, a minority is encouraged to use national resources in pursuit of personal advance.

The new rich inhabit a world apart from the Egyptian masses. The estates, shopping malls, leisure centres and universities of New Cairo (east of the city) and 6 October City (to the west) are guarded by private corporations. Here the riot police of Egypt's vast apparatus of public order are hardly visible. In the city proper, police are everywhere: in popular quarters, in industrial zones and in most public spaces the mass of people are under surveillance and increasingly likely to fall foul of security agencies accustomed to act with impunity. So, too, in rural areas, where for years police have been engaged in suppressing peasant resistance; more recently they have enforced numerous de-sequestration orders, forcibly evicting tenant farmers. Over the last decade much agricultural land has been restored to private owners or to families which held control before the reforms of the Nasser period. Subsequent evictions of fellahin, together with policies which prioritise cash crops for export rather than production of staple foods, have increased migration from rural communities. In major cities the impact is striking: Greater Cairo has spread beyond ring roads which, in the 1990s, cut new routes through desert and untouched farmland. Mile after mile of congested informal housing accommodates millions of people who have moved from the countryside. In 2005 Cairo was said officially to have 15 million inhabitants (Rashed 2005); informal estimates put numbers at up to 22 million, making Cairo a global 'megacity' comparable to giants such São Paulo or Mexico City. It is now home to one in four Egyptians.

Disasters

UN–Habitat estimates that 40 per cent of urban dwellers in Egypt are located in informal areas, many concentrated in 'slum pockets' in which life is particularly precarious.[7] Here millions live in 'working poverty', either partly employed or employed at rates which do not provide income above $2 a day.[8] The International Labour Organisation (ILO) notes that the Middle East and North Africa have the lowest public employment-to-population rates in the world, largely a result of low participation in the workforce by women and youth, with the result that in impoverished areas there are intense pressures upon adult breadwinners (ILO 2009: 12).

The UN also points to increasing problems of environmental degradation and physical safety (UN–Habitat, n.d.). Vast areas of informal housing have been constructed without adequate infrastructure and without supervision, with the result that buildings collapse because of inappropriate design, misuse of materials and/or corrupt relationships among property developers and officials. In both 2007 and 2008 scores of people were killed in Alexandria when apartment blocks collapsed abruptly. In 2008 a rockfall in the Cairo district of Duweiqa killed over a hundred residents living in slum housing: local people blamed the effects of uncontrolled property development nearby. While nervous ministers attacked each other, attempting to deflect criticisms that their departments had been implicated in corrupt dealings, Duweiqa was flooded with police in efforts to inhibit protest. So, too, in the case of an extensive fire in the central Cairo district of Sayyida Zeinab in 2007: after 300 shacks had been destroyed, leaving 1,000 people homeless, protestors were attacked by riot police (Leila 2007).

Fires, train crashes, traumatic failures in buildings, industrial accidents and catastrophes at sea fuel public anger vis-à-vis those in authority, who are often implicated but appear to be immune to successful prosecution. Between 1995 and 2006 there were twenty train crashes, some involving scores of victims (Rashed 2006). In 2006 more than 1,000 people drowned when a ferry from Saudi Arabia sank en route to the port of Safaga – the fourth such disaster since 1994. The ship's owner, who fled to Britain after the incident, is an Egyptian business magnate; he is also a member of the upper house of parliament and of the ruling NDP. He was acquitted of manslaughter – a verdict widely seen as proof that the corporate and governmental elite stand outside the law.

When in 2008 fire destroyed much of a building in Cairo that accommodates the Upper House, some public figures commented that politicians had at last been compelled to experience what many Egyptians endure. Opposition MP Hamdeen Sabahi observed: 'There is a general sense of *Schadenfreude* and anger towards the regime and a feeling that officials deserve what happened' (El-Din 2008).

Desperate migrants

More Egyptians feel compelled to leave the country and more face new dangers as they travel abroad. During the 1970s and 1980s many Egyptians migrated for work, especially in Libya and the Gulf states. When in the 1990s job opportunities in the region decreased sharply, some began to move further afield. The Land Center for Human Rights (LCHR), an NGO based in Cairo, suggests that increasing numbers of Egyptians have been migrating directly to Europe, often using risky, irregular routes which bypass migration controls imposed

by states of the European Union (EU). Thousands are said to have
died en route, some having drowned while attempting crossings of
the Mediterranean. The Center suggests a direct link between the
regime's economic policy, especially changes imposed in rural areas,
and the fate of these migrants:

> Conditions started to deteriorate with the application of Law 96/1992
> [providing for de-sequestration] which was put into action in 1997 and
> resulted in the expulsion of almost one million tenant farmers from
> lands. That accordingly meant that at least seven million people – the
> families of the expelled tenant farmers – have been suffering the double
> onslaught of unemployment and poverty in villages nationwide....
> Immigrants will find a million ways to reach their destination because
> they are desperate.[9]

Hamood (2006) shows that there has been accelerated movement of
poor Egyptians to Europe, that many use smuggling networks and that
they feature prominently among those detained within and deported
from the EU. Like migrants from a host of impoverished African
countries who also use irregular routes, Egyptians feel 'despair and
frustration' and have become increasingly willing to risk all to reach
their destinations (Hamood 2006: 60).

Repression

Part of the despair felt by many Egyptians is associated with increased
vulnerability to abuse at the hands of the state. When in April 2008
thousands of people in the city of Mehalla al-Kubra protested over deteriorating living conditions they met a violent response. Scores were
seized by police: when forty-nine were later tried in the Emergency
Supreme State Security Court several testified that they had been
tortured by officers of State Security. Amnesty International (2008)
described them as 'scapegoats used by the authorities to hide [the
government's] inability to adequately handle the Mahalla protests'.
    Those who challenge NDP control are punished by the state:
political activists are intimidated and many are jailed and tortured.
Local officials and police routinely prohibit opposition meetings,
exclude candidates, buy votes, stuff ballot boxes, manipulate results,
and unleash violence in and around polling stations. In March 2008
Human Rights Watch (2008) described the arrest and detention of

hundreds of opposition candidates as 'a shameless bid to fix the upcoming elections. President Mubarak apparently believes that the outcome of the elections cannot be left up to voters.' The outcome is a crisis of representation which has become the key feature of national politics, stimulating renewed anger and impatience.

Squeezed between the rock of inequality and the hard place of repression, are the mass of Egyptians at breaking point? Are their political organisations (most banned, or semi-legal) able to take the initiative? Is the regime prepared to crush renewed resistance? What are the implications in Egypt and the region?

A moment of change?

Most recent academic literature on Egypt focuses on 'elite politics' – on the state and its dealings with parties of the political establishment.[10] These analyses offer valuable insights but have largely failed to address events which, since the new millennium, warrant a focus on 'politics from below' – the activities of grassroots agents in reacting to and shaping change. This book sets out to address the deficit.

The year 2000 marked a rupture with long-established trends. After a short economic boom in the late 1990s headline growth slowed and the government adopted more aggressive structural adjustment measures, floating the Egyptian pound against the US dollar and speeding up privatisation – a trend fortified by a cabinet of technocrats and businessmen inaugurated in 2004. These policies had their impact on the majority of Egyptians and played a role in stimulating all manner of protests and demands – over availability of bread, access to water and the cost of living. At the same time, intense frustration with the politics of autocracy produced novel political initiatives. During the 1990s it had seemed that popular engagement in politics – what Egyptians call the politics of 'the street' – was characterised by passivity and hesitancy. In September 2000, however, a new series of protests began, initially in support of the Palestinian intifada. Each wave of activity has been followed by another, each giving impetus to further struggles. Support for Palestine brought huge street protests and campaigns for donation and boycott; when these subsided further protests began over the US-led invasion of Iraq. The pattern continued: the pro-democracy movement and the judges' movement of

2004 to 2006 involved many middle-class people and political activists from across the spectrum, including from the (still illegal) Muslim Brotherhood. And in 2006 major strikes began – the most important workers' mobilisations for over five decades.

Not all these movements and groups have been able to build effective constituencies; some have remained marginal and none, with the exception of the textile workers, can claim a decisive victory. But together they have succeeded in changing the agenda for political action under conditions of sustained authoritarianism. The pro-democracy movement defied repression to restore traditions of public dissent and street protest. During elections in 2005 the Muslim Brotherhood secured its largest presence in Parliament, notwithstanding unfair processes and intense violence on the part of the state. The workers of Mehalla al-Kubra and later the tax agency employees initiated a wave of strikes and sit-ins that posed serious problems for those in authority. For the first time judges spoke out against electoral fraud and for independence of the judiciary, and independent newspapers and blogs became key means by which a host of atrocities – from torture of civilians in police stations to electoral malpractice and imprisonment of political activists – received public exposure. Multiple voices of dissent have been heard, creating ripple effects that have stimulated successive collective actions and disturbed the comfortable monopoly of public politics enjoyed by the elite.

This is not to suggest that the regime has lost its grip on power, nor that its commitment to neoliberal principles is faltering. Mubarak and his officials show high levels of resilience. The president has secured a fifth term in office (due to end in 2011), and privatisation schemes and drastic cuts in welfare continue at an unprecedented pace. Repression has intensified. A large group of workers and other protestors from Mehalla al-Kubra has been tried and sentenced by special courts operated under emergency legislation. Bloggers have been seized and held without charge. Leaders of the Muslim Brotherhood (including Khairat El-Shater, its deputy general guide) have been convicted by a military tribunal and sentenced to terms of imprisonment of up to seven years. The notorious Emergency Law, which gives security agencies authority to detain without charge or trial, has been renewed until 2010, despite sustained demands to abolish it and an undertaking from the president (issued as part of an electoral campaign) that he would so do. Civil society associations are still governed by laws that give the executive authority to dissolve any organization, and under which two NGOs (the Labour Rights Centre and the Legal Support Centre) have been dissolved. Four editors-in-chief of independent newspapers have faced trial and the regime has equipped itself with new powers to close satellite television channels. Systematic use of torture against political activists continues and is used increasingly against ordinary citizens.

The regime and its model of control have nonetheless been challenged. For the first time in decades those in power have been confronted by diverse forms of action: protests about water and bread; village mobilisations against de-sequestration; street demonstrations for democracy; solidarity marches and convoys for Palestine; campus protests over war and repression; sit-ins by state employees; strikes in industry; and a host of actions by judges, teachers, university professors, physicians and pharmacists. Millions of Egyptians have participated.

Divided opposition

The biggest challenge for those who wish for change is continued fragmentation of the political opposition, and the absence of effective collaborations that channel energies and provide viable alternatives. Brumberg (2002: 61) writes of 'liberalized autocracy', in which those in power 'strive to pit one group against another in ways that maximize the rulers' room for maneuver and restrict the opposition's capacity to work together'. Egypt might be considered a classic case: the opposition is divided and continues to be limited in effectiveness.

These problems are not unique. In many societies of the Global South people confronted by authoritarian rule struggle to find new means of expressing and realising their aspirations. Egypt is an excellent site for understanding these challenges. Recent developments should prompt us to reconsider the idea that democratisation is primarily about 'regime change' and that democratic transitions proceed by linear means. They emphasise the complexity of state–society relations and the emergence of actors who fall outside the rigid boundaries of 'political society'. One of the objectives of this book is therefore to understand socio-political transformations by addressing the relations that underlie them, rather than by reference to the poles of 'democracy' and 'authoritarianism'. The aim is to examine opportunities and constraints for collective action in the context of neoliberal authoritarian rule, and their effects on the reconfiguration of this context – of which the regime itself is a part.

Structure and aims

The eight chapters which follow examine developments which have shaped the current crisis, producing intense anger and frustration among the mass of people, together with political challenges which opposition movements have yet to overcome.

Chapter 1, 'State and society', considers relations between those in power and the mass of Egyptian society. It asks who rules Egypt and how their authority is assured by a machinery of state which has become increasingly violent and invasive.

Chapter 2, 'Economic policy: from state control to decay and corruption', considers how economic policy has been reshaped since the 1960s, generalising corrupt practices and facilitating rapid enrichment of a minority of Egyptians.

Chapter 3, 'The land and the people', addresses changes which have brought conflict to the countryside as land reforms of the Nasser era have been reversed and commercialisation has taken hold.

Chapter 4, 'Workers' struggles under "socialism" and neoliberalism', considers the context for revival of the workers' movement, examining a complex record of accommodation and confrontation between workers and the state since the Nasser period.

Chapter 5, 'The democracy movement: cycles of protest', addresses the social and political activism of the past decade and the 'spillover' effects that have maintained its momentum.

Chapter 6, 'Islamism(s) old and new', considers the key characteristics of political Islam, the most influential force in contemporary Egyptian politics.

Chapter 7, 'Torture: a state policy', asks why violent abuse has become widespread in the security services and examines the consequences for ordinary Egyptians.

And finally, Chapter 8, 'Mubarak in the international arena', considers outcomes of the regime's foreign policy for domestic politics, examining feedback mechanisms and their implications for those in power. Each chapter examines a specific set of issues. Each is also written with an awareness of the complexity of contemporary Egyptian society: the interconnectedness of economic structures and state–society relations; the multiplicity of social and political actors; the character of power dynamics in an authoritarian system; and the convergence and divergence of varying forms of resistance. The editors believe that a major impediment to understanding such developments in Egypt and other societies of the Global South has been a division between activist/subject, on the one hand, and scholar/researcher/expert, on the other. The binary of those who are 'doing', while others are analysing and interpreting, means that much can be lost 'in translation'.

Contributors to this volume are therefore either activists engaged with the phenomena they discuss or are closely connected to events through extensive personal observation and ties with the people they write about. Understanding that narratives represent objects and also shape them, our intention in this volume is to document a significant moment in modern Egyptian history and to contribute in a modest way to the process of change.

I

State and society

Philip Marfleet

The comedy classic film *Al-Irhab wa'l Kebab* (Terrorism and Kebab) tells the story of an Egyptian everyman lost in the corridors of the giant Mugamma building in Cairo, the headquarters for much of the country's administration. Bullied by government officials and sent helplessly from office to office to resolve a minor problem, he meets other wronged citizens and finally becomes leader of an imagined people's rebellion. The enduring popularity of the film is itself an insight into relations between the state and the people in contemporary Egypt. For the mass of Egyptians, *al-nizam* (the order/ the system) is a controlling influence in everyday life. Notwithstanding decades of rhetoric about democratic opening and liberalisation, Egyptians are ruled by an ultra-authoritarian regime which brooks no opposition. Fifteen years after the release of Sherif Arafa's film, people still laugh at its unlikely hero and the figures of authority he confounds. Their mirth is mixed with desperation, however. Egypt is an increasingly unequal society in which more people are poor and insecure, and in which problems of daily survival are more pressing. The people and 'the order' are joined by little except mutual fear and hostility.

At various points over the past hundred years the mass of Egyptians have played a key role in shaping relations with those in authority. After the First World War the level of protest against European rule was so intense that a British historian of the period describes a 'revolutionary' situation in which activists created local 'republican governments' and some villages set up 'soviets';[1] thirty years later sustained strikes and the demands of 'the street' facilitated a military coup which succeeded in removing occupation forces. But during fifty years of independence, successive regimes – using techniques of both coercion and co-optation – have excluded the people from national politics. Intermittent periods of intense industrial action have sometimes been combined with mass protests, extracting major concessions from those in power. At the same time these episodes have spurred Egypt's rulers to intensify repression, so that relations with the mass of society have become more tense and mistrustful – a development recently accentuated by the commitment of those in power to an aggressive policy of personal profit and material advance. The main characteristics of contemporary politics and socio-cultural life (at least in the 'public' sphere) are an acute sense of alienation and growing anger. This chapter considers relations between the state and the people, and how the current regime maintains its power vis-à-vis an angry and frustrated population.

Low-intensity democracy

The Mubarak regime has much in common with other ruling groups across the Global South which practise 'low-intensity democracy'.[2] Most have close ties to the United States and follow policies integral to the Washington Consensus, favouring neoliberal economic reform and tight control over domestic politics. They include governments in Peru, Colombia, South Korea, Morocco, Kenya, Pakistan, Indonesia and the Philippines, and in a series of Central American states. In each there have been periods of political 'opening'; in each, reform has been superficial. Elections take place, sometimes contested by a plurality of parties and with the involvement of media which are notionally free. But systemic fraud and ballot-rigging, combined with more or less open violence vis-à-vis opposition groups and the media, ensure that power remains within a network of privilege, often closely linked to the armed forces.

Egypt is among the more repressive of these regimes. Its 'democracy' is of such low intensity as to be barely detectable. Officially the government is committed to 'democratic development... deepening of democratic practice, enhancing freedoms and laying down the state of law, institutions and respect of human rights' (State Information Service 2006). Much of its energy, however, is devoted to ballot-rigging, intimidation and electoral fraud. For many years opposition parties and human rights organisations have alleged blatant interference at the polls, recording numerous episodes in which voters have been prevented from polling by the ubiquitous Amn al-Markazi – Central Security, Egypt's riot police. Among incidents reported in 2000 was an attack on voters in the province of Minoufiya, where an opposition candidate had been expected to gather many votes: sixty people were admitted to hospital. A local doctor testified: 'The police opened fire in all directions. They had orders to do that. And they had high orders to prevent people from voting. All the time [there is government talk] about democracy. Where is it?'[3]

During the 2005 parliamentary election people wielding swords and machetes stormed polling stations in Port Said, smuggling in boxes of pre-filled ballots; police meanwhile formed a cordon to prevent voters entering. In Damanhour, 'thugs' were said to have attacked voters, using bayonets, sticks, knives and bottles filled with acid and petrol; the police observed events impassively (Safieddine 2005; Sami 2005).

These practices have embarrassed even the regime's closest allies, who fear an explosion of popular anger which could wreak havoc with their interests in Egypt and the region. In 2008 then-President George W. Bush felt obliged to complain that Mubarak would not permit the most modest political reform, observing (without a hint of irony) that 'too often in the Middle East, politics has consisted of one leader in power and the opposition in jail' (BBC 2008c). Western media which cheer on the regime's economic strategy express dismay at the vulgarity of its repression. For the *Washington Post* Egyptian elections are 'a squalid process' orchestrated by a president of 'martial crudeness' (Diehl 2005). *The Economist* (2008) warns that deficits in political representation could prove disastrous for a regime which has supervised a general crisis of society:

> The fact is that most of Egypt's 75 m[illion] people struggle to get
> by, their ambitions thwarted by rising prices, appalling state schools,
> capricious judges, a plodding and corrupt bureaucracy and a cronyist
> regime that pretends democracy but in fact crushes all challengers

and excludes all participation. The visitor might well conclude that by damming up the normal flow of politics, Egypt's rulers risk bringing on a deluge.

The journal asks: 'will the dam burst?' (*Economist* 2008).

Inequality and change

Many Egyptians – perhaps the majority – live at the margin of survival, dependent upon the few staple foods that still enjoy state subsidy. Changes in price or fluctuations in supply have immediate consequences: in December 2007 the Ministry of Social Solidarity unexpectedly lifted subsidies on some grades of flour, leading to shortages of bread and bitter arguments among those desperate for *aysh baladi*, the loaves which sustain most urban Egyptian families. One local newspaper led its story on 'the bread queue crisis' by quoting a Cairene woman: 'We will soon kill and steal from each other for bread. Where is the country going?' (Nafie 2007). Over the next four months, at least eleven people were killed during conflicts at bakeries (Johnstone 2008).

According to the World Bank the inequality gap is widening. In 1991 the poorest 10 per cent of the population had access to 3.9 per cent of the country's income; the richest 20 per cent received 26.7 per cent. Ten years later, the poorest 10 per cent had access to 3.7 per cent of national income; the richest received 29.5 per cent.[4] These headline figures do not fully capture the reality of recent change, however. Thirty years of economic reform have encouraged private capitalists who during the 1970s were known as the 'fat cats'. They have since been indulged with all manner of concessions including, since 2004, cuts of over 50 per cent in the rate of corporation tax. One outcome is a pattern of social development extreme even by the standards of the poorest regions of the Global South. It is especially glaring in Cairo, where residents of areas such as Misr al-Gedida (Heliopolis), Zamalek and Ma'adi live in glitzy tower blocs and villas alongside marbled shopping malls: nearby in Zeitoun, Bulak Abu al-'Ela or Dar al-Salaam, people are crowded into slum zones in which daily life is ever more precarious. Abaza, who has studied the new urban culture, observes: 'Cairo consists largely of slums. It is the culture of slums opposite a culture of international hotels and shopping malls.

I see an increasing contradiction ... you are raising up expectations, dreams and desires.'⁵

Nader Fergany, lead author of the UN's *Arab Human Development Report*, suggests that government policy has produced inequalities not seen since the colonial era:

> There's a vicious circle of a small clique getting filthy rich and the rest getting impoverished... We have returned this country to what it used to be before the 1952 revolution: the 1 per cent society. One per cent controls almost all the wealth of the country.⁶

In the 1950s and 1960s Egypt had been a model for radical change across the 'Third' world. President Gamal Abdel-Nasser declared for socialism, initiating a (limited) land reform, nationalisations of commerce and industry, and elaborate programmes of welfare and public education (Ayubi 1991). The contrast with recent policies is sharp and has led to increasing nostalgia among many Egyptians about the old order. But the core of the Nasserist state is still intact – and has indeed been integral to processes that have produced today's crisis.

In the 1950s Egypt was among many states of Africa and the Middle East in which anti-colonial movements brought to power 'new men' formally committed to African/Arab 'socialism'. After years of rising protest against colonial occupation, in 1952 the Free Officers finally deposed a pro-British monarchy and announced an agenda for radical change. Nasser and his colleagues were not *representatives* of the anti-colonial protest movement that preceded 1952, however. They did not emerge directly from the ranks of the activists, nor were they accountable to any of the key political currents within it. They owed their opportunity to the failure of established political organisations to challenge the *ancien régime* and the forces of occupation. Mohamed Hassanein Heikal, a Nasser loyalist who became the country's leading journalist and commentator, suggests that the Officers 'only acted to fill a void'.⁷ They were in fact radical conspirators – a group of nationalists within the officer corps frustrated by the inability of others to strike a decisive blow against colonialism. Most were opposed to mass political engagement, including involvement of their subordinates in the armed forces: Baker (1978: 25) comments that 'There was to be no revolutionary disruption of the ranks. From its inception the Free Officers movement was elitist, even within the military context.'

When the group launched a *coup d'état* the monarchy collapsed, its downfall so swift that the Officers were uninterested in even token support in the streets. The group went on to organise its activities secretly, avoiding formal links with civilian allies and reacting to popular manifestations of enthusiasm and further demands for change sceptically and even violently. Among its first initiatives was suppression of a strike in the city of Kafr al-Dawwar and the execution of two of the workers' leaders.[8] Its early policies were contradictory: a land reform introduced in 1952 was said to be a 'revolutionary' measure but affected less than 10 per cent of cultivable land and allowed many large landowners to retain control of their estates (Ansari 1986: 79). It nonetheless succeeded in stimulating enormous expectations among the fellahin: 'peasants deluded themselves into thinking they were entering a revolutionary stage ... many stopped paying dues ... many declared that the army gave them the lands'. The Officers responded with calls to resist 'extremists' (Ansari 1986: 80).

Years of rising expectation had created pressures that the Officers could not resist. They struggled to deliver welfare promises whilst restraining the movement that had facilitated their rise to power and that now continued to seek wide-ranging change. The imperative of control was decisive and soon a new political formation was in evidence – one in which senior military men and technocrats were dominant. They declared for state socialism, anti-imperialism, non-alignment and for commitment to an independent 'third' world. The state itself – led by the army – would enact progress, they maintained, using further agrarian reform, nationalisations of foreign capital and assets, and control of trade to modernise Egyptian society. Landowners, merchants and entrepreneurs of the colonial era were indeed forced to accept a reduced status, though significantly they remained part of the networks of influence: Zaalouk (1989: 41) comments that they became a lobby for private capital *within* a new 'state bourgeoisie'.

Nasser stimulated much personal loyalty: he was identified with removal of the monarchy; the expulsion of occupation forces; land reform; industrialisation; nationalisation of the Suez Canal and subsequent humiliation of Britain, France and Israel; and the Palestinian cause. At the same time he alienated each and every political current that enjoyed genuine relationships with the people, including the Communists and the Muslim Brotherhood, whose activists were incarcerated and tortured and among whom some were executed. Increasingly he ruled by concentrating power among a small group of loyalists within the armed forces, and by controlling the new corporations and co-operatives which now dominated economic affairs. He expanded the police and intelligence apparatus, developing a network of informers which monitored workplaces and communities on the model of the Stalinist state. In the late 1960s came an inevitable break, as the patience of the mass of Egyptians was finally exhausted. When the army failed catastrophically during the 1967 war with Israel, workers and students demanded change: the regime itself had failed, they argued, and it was time for the people to participate in shaping an alternative. The former communist Anouar Abdel-Malik argued that the Officers betrayed those who had ushered them to power. Egypt had fallen into the hands of 'a devouring bureaucracy... let loose with the immunity of autocracy'; the people had been subordinated to the interests of a military-bureaucratic elite which 'determined the objectives and modes of national action': the people were present merely 'to supply the manpower' (Abdel-Malik 1968: 366).

Infitah and after

This was the system inherited by President Anwar al-Sadat on Nasser's death in 1970. He soon used the apparatus of repression to marginalise powerful rivals and, bolstered by partial military success in the 1973 conflict with Israel, launched a programme of radical economic change – the *infitah* ('opening'). This aimed to reinstate the private sector and to attract foreign capital. Businessmen who had left Egypt for the Gulf states were urged to return and facilitate new relations with economies of the West. Meanwhile Sadat encouraged a 'de-Nasserisation' campaign, through which his own supporters attacked the repression of the former regime and argued for political reform.

Initially *infitah* brought rapid change. There was a surge in imports as for the first time in over twenty years consumer goods produced aboard entered Egypt freely. Arab and Western businessmen arrived with what Baker (1978: 143) calls '"gold rush" excitement', prompting a property boom. Leading members of the regime assured them that change was to be permanent: the role of the state would be reduced and private capital would be encouraged by all means. In fact there was little meaningful investment from abroad and many business adventurers promptly retreated. Meanwhile conditions of the mass of people deteriorated: in 1976 one estimate suggested that 80 per cent of the population were worse off than when the new policy had been announced just three years earlier.[9] The main beneficiaries had been commission agents and profiteers:

> Contractors, real-estate speculators, and merchants flourished on the economic boom: importers, partners and agents of foreign firms, tourist operators, lawyers and middlemen who helped investors negotiate bureaucratic tangles, thrived on the cuts they took from the resource inflow... Officials reaped commissions on state contracts and engaged in widespread corrupt practices. Together, these groups were forming a 'parasitic bourgeoisie' living off *Infitah.* (Hinnebusch 1985: 69–70)

These were the 'fat cats' targeted in 1977, when huge demonstrations – 'food riots' – challenged Sadat's attempt to reduce subsidies on staple foods and fuel, as directed by his new allies in the USA and by the IMF. Millions of people protested and in Cairo symbols of the new wealth – luxury hotels, boutiques, nightclubs and casinos – were ransacked and burned. Sadat had not created a new 'parasitic' class, however; rather, he had opened opportunities for private capitalists tolerated under the Nasserist state and among whom some had seized opportunities for enrichment. Together with *arrivistes* among the building contractors, property dealers and traders encouraged by liberalisation, they gained entry into a network of interests in which senior military figures and bureaucrats made common cause with business and commerce.

On Sadat's death in 1981 Mubarak picked up the baton. He, too, pursued a strategy that combined market reform with careful nurturing of state interests – what he called a 'productive *infitah*', which he promised would bring the benefits of liberal capitalism without the speculative excesses of the previous decade. But the regime was moving far too slowly for the taste of the USA and the IMF. They wanted a programme of change that was both faster and broader – to align Egypt with the agenda for neoliberal reform being imposed across the Global South. Observing these pressures, Springborg (1989: 257) commented on the 'missionary zeal' of Western advisers and officials working with the Egyptian state:

They believe that by forcing Egypt to accept the growth of the new orthodoxy they will save it from itself. By encouraging the growth of the private at the expense of the public sector, by forcing relaxation of controls over producers, especially those in agriculture, by inducing economic decision makers to devalue the currency, raise interest rates and rationalize consumer subsidies, they will help establish an economically viable, productive and ultimately more independent Egypt.

In the face of a growing debt crisis and strongly encouraged by an increasingly confident business lobby Mubarak acceded to many of the IMF's demands, all the while protecting the interests of his bedrock support – the officer corps and the cadre of senior officials which gave continuity with the Nasserist era.[10] The outcome was a state which combined centralised control over economic and political affairs with encouragement for private capital at the highest level, including within the apparatus of state itself. By the mid-1990s, suggest Henry and Springborg (2001: 155), Egypt was in the grip of 'a nexus of cronies, officers, bureaucrats and public sector managers'.

Cohabitation of private and public interests produced apparently contradictory outcomes. As Mitchell (2002: 241) demonstrates, US aid which had been provided with the formal aim of assisting private enterprise and 'pluralism' in fact strengthened the role of the state, notably of the military, which developed a major presence in manufacturing, agriculture and construction: as early as the mid-1980s the Food Security Division of the armed forces had become the largest agro-industrial complex in the country (Mitchell 2002: 241). Meanwhile, senior state officials entered business partnerships in which their influence guaranteed preferences or even monopolies in the local market – and rapid enrichment. By the 1990s senior members of the regime were among Egypt's leading businessmen – either through direct personal involvement or through close family connections. In 2006 Kifaya, a key organisation within the democracy movement, produced a report on *Corruption in Egypt: A Black Cloud That Never Passes*.[11] It alleged that the president's sons received payments for facilitating activities of foreign corporations and that a series of top officials, some associated with the Mubarak family, benefited from similar deals. Egypt should be renamed *Fasadistan* – 'land of corruption'- Kifaya suggested.[12]

Repression and co-optation

It is this closely networked group that controls the apparatus of state, *al-nizam*, the political order which subordinates the mass of Egyptians. Its combination of crude repression with more subtle methods of co-optation and patronage reflects the practices of successive post-colonial regimes.

Nasser penalised all dissident activity, jailing large numbers of political activists and eventually reducing the energies of the mass movement that had facilitated his rise to power. During the turbulent 1970s Sadat had much greater difficulty containing dissent; he ordered military intervention to suppress the protests of 1977 and later launched an assault on radical activists he blamed for the events, jailing thousands and forcing many more into hiding. He declared: 'The next time I'm going to be ten times as ruthless.'[13] When in 1981 Sadat was assassinated by an Islamist army officer, Mubarak declared a National Emergency, which has since been renewed continuously, so that Egypt has been ruled under special powers for over twenty-five years, during which the regime has consolidated a vast apparatus of repression.

Today the Ministry of the Interior has hundreds of thousands of special police and security agents, including the ubiquitous riot police of the Amn al-Markazi (Central Security), Mabaheth Amn al-Dawla (General Directorate of State Security Investigations) and Jihaz Amn al-Dawla (State Security Service), together with a huge network of informers. The intelligence services also boast a bloated apparatus of parallel and sometimes competing organisations, including Mukhabarat al-Aama (General Intelligence and Security Service); Mukhabarat al-Harbeya (Military Intelligence Service); and Jihaz al-Amn al-Qawmi (National Security Service). With basic rights suspended under the Emergency Law they act at will: free to arrest suspects and detain them without court order or trial; to refer civilians to military courts at which there is no right of appeal; to ban strikes, demonstrations and public meetings of more than ten individuals; and to censor or close newspapers. Ostensibly their target is the Islamist opposition, especially organisations which, in the 1980s and 1990s, mounted armed attacks on police and civilians. But when in 1999 Islamist leaders abandoned their militant strategy the Emergency continued, becoming what Human Rights Watch (2003) calls 'an Emergency without end'. The regime had become habituated to powers which were no longer exceptional measures but routine means of maintaining social control.

All manner of people have been seized and imprisoned arbitrarily: students, journalists, bloggers, political activists, industrial militants and peasants who resist land seizures or evictions. Some 'disappear' and are discovered later in offices of the intelligence services, in police stations or prisons. In December 2008 a group of young men, including bloggers and student activists, went missing from their homes; when arrest warrants were eventually issued security agencies refused to reveal where they were being held. A human rights lawyer said: 'Egypt's young people are being detained without a legal basis... Their lives are in danger because we have no idea where they are – even the public prosecution office doesn't know where they are. This is state thuggery' (Carr 2008).

Electoral farce

The current regime treats electoral exercises with contempt. In 2005 judges reported systematic abuse of the voting system during a national referendum on constitutional change. According to the government, 54 per cent of registered voters turned out to approve its proposals with a vote of over 80 per cent in favour. The Judges' Club (Nadi al-Quda) declared that voter turnout was no more than 3 per cent; it also used photographs and videos to show that government officials at the polls completed 'yes' ballots and excluded forms on which voters had indicated 'no' (Human Rights Watch 2005b).[14] During both presidential and parliamentary elections which took place a few months later, journalists from Egypt and abroad who attempted to report on polling were attacked by police and plainclothes security officers. According to Yehia Qallash, secretary of the Press Syndicate in Cairo, the frequency of such attacks has been increasing: 'Each incident is followed by flimsy investigations and meagre attempts to bring those responsible to justice', he says.[15] Government promises to allow more freedom of speech are 'lip service'.[16]

The regime's particular difficulty during elections is its inability to demonstrate even modest evidence of popular support. Mubarak's ruling NDP is a shell organisation – a network of appointed agents and officials inseparable from the national and local machinery of the state. It maintains complex relations of patronage which reach from the president down to the village level. Governors of the twenty-seven major administrative units (governorates) are appointed by the president; they in turn appoint officials in regions, districts, cities and villages (in 1994 the government ended a centuries-old tradition of local democracy whereby villages had elected mayors and deputy mayors). The entire national hierarchy is controlled through the Ministry of the Interior, with the NDP operating as a shadow organisation that provides the thinnest veneer of formal democracy but that has no popular base or means of positive mobilisation. During elections its officials transport state employees en masse to polling stations to vote as directed, usually under threat of transfer, demotion or worse, while voters not employed by the state are often offered a small fee to ballot as directed. By such means improbably generous votes are recorded for NDP candidates, while opposition parties apparently register insignificant support.

Despite widespread cynicism about the polls, voters (especially those with specific political allegiances) make sustained attempts to participate in the electoral process. In 2005 candidates of the Muslim Brotherhood won large votes in early rounds of the general election; in a third round, huge numbers of riot police were deployed in many areas, with the express aim of preventing electors reaching polling stations.[17] Not all the regime's methods are based upon physical coercion, however: Kassem (2004: 7) comments that for many years Mubarak has used 'a mixture of fear and rewards' to co-opt the main opposition parties and to render ineffective key organisations such as trade unions and professional syndicates. This approach also has its roots in corporatist strategies developed under the Nasser and Sadat regimes.

'Pointless parties'

In 1953 Nasser established a single legal political organisation, the Liberation Rally. He declared: 'The Liberation Rally is not a political party. Its creation was prompted by the desire to establish a body that would organize the people's forces and overhaul the social set-up.'[18] This reflected Nasser's elitism and deep mistrust of independent collective organisation: Baker (1978: 94) describes the Rally as 'an instrument for depoliticizing Egypt public life', a means of inhibiting the activity of trade unions, of rural collectives that had emerged in response to land reform, and of communist and Islamist organisations. It was replaced in 1956 by the National Union, a token body through which Egyptians were to solidarise during the Suez conflict with Britain, France and Israel. In 1962 this, too, was abandoned in favour of the Arab Socialist Union (ASU), a body which initially resembled a conventional party, with mass membership (in theory the bulk of the adult population) and branches in villages, city districts, workplaces and educational institutions. But the Union was also run autocratically by the military elite and by senior bureaucrats: in 1965 Nasser admitted, 'The fact is we have no internal organization, except on the books.'[19] The ASU did, however, provide mechanisms for co-opting dissidents who survived Nasser's intensive repression. The clearest example was the Egyptian Communist Party, which dissolved itself in 1964, with leading members joining the Union and receiving token positions of authority.

In the mid-1970s Sadat undertook a democratic 'opening', permitting the establishment of 'platforms' (initially called *manabir* – 'pulpits') within the ASU – groupings which, he said, would represent the range of views across Egyptian society. In 1978 he announced the establishment of the NDP, launched with the motto 'Food for every mouth, a house for every individual, and prosperity for all.'[20] Sadat declared that it would be an example of revolutionary purity: 'In all of history I cannot find an example of such totally democratic action as we have taken in establishing the NDP.'[21] The new party absorbed the entire leadership of the ASU: in effect the government moved en bloc to an organisation which inherited control of the armed forces and the bureaucracy. A further group within the ASU eventually became the New Wafd ('Delegation') Party, which claimed the legacy of nationalist resistance and of the liberal era of the early twentieth century, while remnants of the Egyptian Communist Party and Nasserite nationalists became the National Progressive Unionist Party (usually known as al-Tagammu').

The multi-party system has since expanded from Sadat's three organisations to twenty-four: none, however, enjoys political independence. Those who wish to establish new organisations must apply to a Committee for Affairs of Political Parties, undertaking to play by formal and informal rules of which the most important is an agreement never to mobilise publicly. Mass rallies, lobbies, marches, demonstrations or similar forms of collective political action involving these organisations are rare: most opposition parties have never undertaken a major public initiative and, with repeated renewals of the Emergency, are unlikely to do so. Their leaders have long adopted a meek, quiescent role, accepting that the price of legality is marginalisation.[22] Rif'at al-Said, leader of al-Tagammu', recognises that mainstream parties 'represent nothing in Egyptian politics and have no standing whatsoever with the Egyptian people'.[23] In an unusually frank – even bizarre – admission, he continues:

> Do not believe any person who says that the Nasserite Party is a real party, or that the Progressive Unionist Party, the National Democratic Party, the Muslim Brothers, nor the Islamic groups are parties in the true sense of the term... All these are just groupings of individuals floating on the surface of society.

Independent candidates have sometimes attempted to break the mould, using elections as an activist platform. Invariably they are the target of police interventions. Like the NDP most are shadow organisations; only the Muslim Brotherhood, which is still illegal, has an active and engaged national membership (see Chapter 6). But its leaders also hesitate to bring their supporters openly onto the political stage: even in the face of extreme provocation by the regime the Brotherhood adopts a restrained approach in which protest is no more than 'symbolic'.[24] In an assessment of political developments during 2008, the Cairo newspaper *Al-Ahram Weekly* characterised all these organisations as 'pointless parties' paralysed by factionalism (El-Nahas 2009). It added:

> Ferocious power struggles over leading party posts are now the norm while any agenda promoting political reform has sunk without trace. Accusations of maintaining close connections with the government were repeatedly levelled at party leaders. Beyond holding occasional seminars and endlessly issuing statements, Egypt's political parties did little. Hardly surprising, then, that their mostly deserted offices and unreadable mouthpieces are generally viewed as pointless by the public. (El-Nahas 2009)

The hand of the regime can be detected in many internal party battles, suggested the newspaper. The organisations' collective paralysis, however, is an outcome of general sterility – the absence of rank-and-file membership, of public activity and of policies relevant to the lives of the mass of people. They remain little more than 'platforms' safely enclosed within a system which has changed little since the time of the ASU.

Corporatism

Decades of repression and co-optation have produced a profound crisis of representation at the level of formal politics. So, too, in industry where trade unions have long been part of the system of patronage (see Chapter 4). Local union representatives are routinely induced to work in the interests of the state. Kassem (2004: 109) notes that union officers elected to company boards can receive up to E£30,000 a month – an income beyond the dreams of most Egyptians. She adds, 'it is common to find individuals who simultaneously represent workers and the state'. Outgoing union officers can automatically become part of the national union apparatus and in effect move into the NDP bureaucracy. In 2004, 21 of 23 heads of the Egyptian Trade Union Federation (ETUF) were NDP members; the president of the federation, Sayyid Rashid, was a veteran member of the ruling party, a member of parliament and deputy speaker of the People's Assembly.

These arrangements originated in the corporatism of the Nasser era. Beinin and Lockman (1987: 444) show how in the 1950s union leaders struck a 'bargain' with President Nasser which was to have historic implications for Egyptian workers. In exchange for confirmation of their own positions and promises of job security for employees in the state sector, labour leaders agreed to support the new regime – 'a military dictatorship that had repeatedly demonstrated its unalterable opposition to a free trade union movement, the right to strike, and any form of independent initiative and action by workers' (Beinin and Lockman 1987: 444). The federation they led soon became part of the state bureaucracy, charged with isolating workers' struggles and inhibiting attempts to organise independently. In addition, in the 1960s committees of the ASU were established in most large workplaces, notionally to facilitate education, but in fact to maintain surveillance of both the workforce and of local managers, whom the regime kept on a short leash, anxious that none should develop their own ambitions. Even the largely loyal Nasserist Mohamed Hassanain Heikal alleged that in industry the ASU had operated primarily as a spy system.[25] For decades the national federation worked to draw local representatives into the networks of privilege, so that workers in struggle discovered they must contest both management and the union. During the 1980s a series of major confrontations revealed the scale of the problem. El Shafei concludes:

> Egyptian trade unions act as agents of the state inside the workers' movement.... Even the lowest level of the trade union bureaucracy – the local union committees – is quite isolated from workers' struggles. Since members of these union committees are nearly powerless vis-à-vis high levels of the trade union structure, they tend to distance themselves from militant workers' actions in order to avoid punishment from their superiors. (El Shafei 1995: 38)

The process of co-optation neutralises local union officers, leaving workers without representation outside immediate rank-and-file groupings, which the security services attempt to disrupt and fragment. The state has found it more difficult to tame the syndicates – the associations of lawyers, doctors, engineers and other professional groups in which opposition organisations, notably the Muslim Brotherhood, have been able to make some progress (see Chapter 6). But here, too, the regime observes and intervenes, sometimes with full force and with the effect of paralysing syndicates for long periods. For more than ten years the Engineers' Association has been under state custody, unable to organise its own elections.

Divided society

Strikes which have affected much of Egyptian industry since 2006 are overwhelmingly 'illegal' – unauthorised by the ETUF. Some have unified workers across the country, producing independent trade-union committees that challenge the authority of the national federation (see Chapter 4). Corporatist arrangements, however, continue to stifle action in many workplaces, bearing down on workers exposed to the full weight of neoliberal economic policy. Meanwhile a minority of Egyptians experience enrichment facilitated by the state itself, the outcome of a process in which growth of private capital has become part of an official agenda within the 'public' sector. Such are the extremes of inequality in today's Egypt that economic journalists draw parallels with the society of Antiquity: according to *The Economist* (2005), the country's capitalist dynasties are 'the new Pharaohs'. Among them is the Sawiris family, owners of Egypt's first multinational corporation, Orascom. Closely associated with the inner circles of the NDP, the family boasts two generations of dollar billionaires whose fortunes compare to those of the oil dynasties of the Gulf; Naguib Sawiris is said to be the third richest individual in the Arab world, ranking behind only the wealthiest men of the Gulf states. Three of the Sawiris clan are among the world's 300 richest individuals: for the first time Egyptians are part of the modern global elite.[26]

Increasingly the nouveau riche opt to live in isolation from the wider society. From the mid-1990s gated communities began to appear in new neighbourhoods constructed on Cairo's desert fringe: here security guards patrol villas with manicured gardens and swimming pools, reached from the city centre by ring roads that avoid the quarters of the poor and give easy access to elite clubs, resorts and marinas on the Mediterranean and Red Sea coasts. Mitchell

Table 1.1   Top ten Arab billionaires (2007)

Rank	Name	Country	Net worth ($ bn)
1	Al Waleed Bin Talal	Saudi Arabia	20.3
2	Nasser Al-Kharafi and family	Kuwait	11.5
3	Naguib Sawiris	Egypt	10.0
4	Mohammed Al Amoudi	Saudi Arabia	8.0
4	Abdul Aziz Al Ghurair and family	UAE	8.0
6	Maan Al Sanea	Saudi Arabia	7.5
7	Sulaiman Al Rajhi	Saudi Arabia	7.4
8	Onsi Sawiris	Egypt	5.0
9	Saleh Al Rajhi	Saudi Arabia	4.4
10	Nassef Sawiris	Egypt	3.9

Source: Forbes Arabia.[27]

notes an apparent contradiction in relation to government policy: while politicians and officials emphasise monetary control and fiscal discipline as means of containing inflation, reducing budget deficits and prompting general growth, there has been an explosion of activity in construction of luxury property. 'The largest real estate explosion Egypt [has] ever seen' has been accompanied by frenetic advertising campaigns urging the rich to invest (Mitchell 2002: 273). The state has been deeply involved, selling public land cheaply and equipping areas around Cairo designated for private development with infrastructure and transport links including expressways and bridges. Between the gated communities are multiplex cinemas, hypermarkets and malls and – barely distinguishable among the mushrooming 'all-sorts' architecture – new university campuses.

The Bahgat Group, which operates Dreamland, west of Cairo, advertises its project as offering 'magnificent views of the Pyramids, [with] golf course, lush green landscapes, swimming pools and artificial lakes'. It is strategically located:

> Dreamland's location was chosen with great care, in order to ensure that the compound is easily accessible from anywhere in Egypt. Dreamland is linked with Cairo via a network of major highways, including Cairo's ring road. This facilitates access from, and to, any other destination in Egypt.[28]

Contrasts with the city's popular quarters could hardly be more striking. *The Economist* notes jarring differences between the new elite communities and 'alleyways of brick tenements where half of Cairo's people actually live', adding that 'the gap between a very rich few and the teeming mass of have-nots [seems] to yawn ever wider' (*The Economist* 2008).

Uprising

The regime sometimes reveals its own anxieties. In 2007 Finance Minister Yousef Boutros-Ghali confided that the plight of the poor was 'a basic challenge that keeps me awake at night'.[29] The 'challenge' is a fear of the masses never far from the thoughts of those in power. For long periods they have been able to exclude the majority of people from political life, but at the cost of accumulating grievances eventually expressed in sudden and explosive outbursts in the

streets and workplaces. In 1968 protests by workers in the industrial
city of Helwan ended a period of passivity which had lasted for
almost fifteen years. Strikes were followed by student demonstrations,
prompting President Nasser to make an unprecedented personal
visit in an attempt to contain the movement.[30] In 1977 Anwar Sadat
retained power by mobilising the armed forces against the '*intifada*
of bread' that challenged cuts to subsidies of food and fuel. In 1984
a powerful local response to similar cuts erupted in the Delta city
of Kafr al-Dawwar: the state again intervened with armed force (see
Chapter 4). In 1986 the Mubarak regime was confronted by a rebellion
among its own footsoldiers – the 'auxiliary forces mutiny' – when
thousands of police conscripts abandoned barracks and marched on
Cairo and Alexandria, destroying many hotels, shops and restaurants
in protest against their slave-like conditions. Once more the regime
was compelled to bring tanks onto the streets to defeat what was, in
effect, an uprising of peasants in uniform.[31]

Each eruption of anger threatens to become another *intifada*,
drawing in millions whose frustrations have reached boiling point.
The events of 1977 were of special significance: demonstrations were
directed against both the regime and the IMF, whose demands to
cut subsidies had produced an overnight reduction in the size of the
(then) one-piastre loaf. Government offices and homes of the elite
were attacked and the president and his family rebuked by name:
popular slogans included, 'Down with Sadat's palaces', and 'Jihan,
Jihan, the People are hungry' (Jihan Sadat, wife of the president).[32]
Such was the scale and energy of the protests that Sadat promptly
revoked the changes, leaving the people with a rare but vital triumph
in their battle with the state. Such events have become part of the
collective memory of the people – and of successive regimes. In 2008
the American Chamber of Commerce in Egypt, a champion of free-
market policy, commented that renewed cuts would indeed produce
social unrest: 'the specter of the 1977 Bread Riots', it observed, 'haunts
government officials' (Bakry 2008).

This is a highly charged and dangerous situation for those in
power, whose anxiety is tangible. In 2007 they reacted nervously to
prolonged protests over acute shortages of drinking water. For several
months demonstrations across the Nile Delta involved large numbers
of the country's poorest people in what Cairo newspapers called a

'revolution of the thirsty'. In some towns thousands blocked roads and demonstrated outside government offices, eventually prompting a personal intervention from the president. Twelve months later there were further protests over water supplies in cities including Suez, Cairo and Giza.

While the state can guarantee to water the gardens of Cairo's elite, it is unable to provide adequate supplies for millions of people (Leila 2008). Further popular struggles may well be stimulated by a pressing need for life's essentials – for bread and for water.

2

Economic policy:
from state control to decay and corruption

Ahmad El-Sayed El-Naggar

In 1974 President Anwar al-Sadat introduced Law 43, initiating a landmark shift in Egyptian economic policy. This reduced taxes and import tariffs for foreign investors and exempted them from key labour laws – a clear indicator that policy was now to be focused on the global market. A stream of legislation followed, facilitating *infitah*, 'the Opening' or 'Open Door' by which Sadat aimed to move from state ownership of strategic industries and a dominant role in service provision and foreign trade towards the free-market model. The current economic and political system in Egypt is an outcome of this strategy.

Over twenty years earlier President Nasser had introduced a land reform and the first moves towards Egyptianisation and nationalisation of the economy. This represented an attempt to change the structure of Egyptian industry by means of direct state intervention, and during the 1950s huge industrial complexes were established, including the Iron and Steel Complex in Helwan, Racta Paper and Nisr Tires in Alexandria, and Kima Fertilizers in Aswan. Following the joint military offensive of Britain, France and Israel in 1956, the government began nationalising enterprises owned by British and French citizens; later it nationalised all foreign assets and large Egyptian private capital. By the end of this process in the mid-1960s the public sector was the dominant economic force, with state ownership contributing 70 per cent of production, employing 50 per cent of the labour force and accounting for 90 per cent of new investment in the industrial sector (PACE 1978: 266). At this stage the role of the state in the Nasserist economic model already exceeded that prescribed by Keynesian models for assuring stability of the national economy.

The Nasserist approach largely matched the theoretical model of state capitalism, one in which the state controls capital accumulation, taking the place of capitalists too weak to accomplish a substantial economic transformation. The outcome was a bureaucratic capitalism in which those in power used public assets for their own interests. The bureaucracy became a closed class, inheriting positions of power and eventually producing a renewed private capitalism.

Infitah paved the way for traditional capitalism to operate in all fields of economic activity. As the capitalist class of the colonial period had been greatly reduced by nationalisation, the first capitalist groups to take advantage of new opportunities in the 1970s were those engaged in illicit activities such as the sale of antiquities, drugs and weapons, or in unofficial currency exchange. Others quickly accumulated wealth through connections with bureaucrats and government officials who sold state-owned agricultural land and real estate at low prices in return for huge commissions. Such mechanisms led to the emergence of a capitalist class loyal to the bureaucratic ruling class – one which initially had no entrepreneurial culture but which profited directly from its links to the state (see Sadowski 1991). In parallel, a class of agricultural capitalists was being re-formed at the expense of small farmers. Early in his presidency Sadat had started to erode the gains of poor and middle-income peasants, beginning a process that was to continue for over thirty years, culminating with the reversal of Nasserist agricultural reform (see Chapter 3).

According to finance minister Yousef Boutros-Ghali, the private sector's contribution to Egypt's GDP rose from 30 per cent in 1991 to 80 per cent in 2006 (Moussa 2006). By 2008 it contributed 100 per cent of agricultural production, 83 per cent of production in manufacturing industry, 92 per cent of the service sector (including health and education) and 93 per cent of activity in wholesale and retail trade services (Egyptian Central Bank 2008: 132). However, this privatised economy had all the features of 'crony capitalism' in which rent-seeking bureaucrats were closely linked to businessmen, and their mutual interests and patronage were reflected in economic policies (Sadowski 1991). Hence, the Egyptian market-oriented economy lacked commitment to practices associated with advanced capitalisms, such as formal guarantees of the rule of law, a fair wage system, or investment in knowledge production through research and development. Economic policy included repeated attempts to radically reduce public spending allocated to subsidising basic commodities, services and social transfers, which had already become one of the lowest worldwide (World Bank 2007b: 194–232).

Economic policy since *infitah*

The policy framework of the Mubarak regime is based on selective choice of free-market principles without concern for social welfare or political reform in the interests of the mass of Egyptians. This accords with the preferences of creditor states and of the IMF, which by the late 1980s held Egyptian debt amounting to some $50 billion (World Bank 1990: 250). By the 1990s the regime was implementing the demands of its creditors without restraint, its inefficiency and corruption making the outcome particularly damaging to the population at large.

Like many of his counterparts in the South, Mubarak has set out to diminish the economic role of the state in all its aspects. The state has ceased from direct investment in industry, agriculture, internal and external trade, limiting its intervention to the provision of infrastructure. It has meanwhile liberalised the financial and currency markets and privatised the public sector, issuing a series of laws and decrees that serve the interests of local and foreign capital while increasing burdens on the Egyptian middle class and the poor. Among many measures which favour private capital, three passed in 2004–5 illustrate the trend.

Taxation: serving the interests of the rich

Egyptian taxation law has long been controversial because most private-sector companies have been able to evade payments. Difficulties in proving tax evasion and meagre penalties for breaking

Table 2.1 Remittances and subsidies, Egypt and selected states (2005)

	Population (m)	GDP (US$)	Public expenditure (US$)	Remittances and subsidies (US$)	Public expenditure as % of GDP	Remittances and subsidies as % of GDP	Remittances and subsidies as % of public expenditure	Per capita share of remittances and subsidies (US$)
Egypt	74	89,369	20,197	3,636	22.6	4.1	18	49
Tunisia	10	28,683	8,462	2,877	29.5	10.0	34	288
Morocco	30	51,621	16,157	3,878	31.3	7.5	24	129
Algeria	33	102,256	24,644	12,322	24.1	12.1	50	373
Norway	5	295,513	100,770	67,516	34.1	22.9	67	13,503
S. Korea	48	787,624	168,552	87,647	21.4	11.1	52	1826
China	1,305	2,234,297	248,007	158,724	11.1	7.1	64	122
S. Africa	47	239,543	70,995	39,707	29.6	16.6	56	845
UK	60	2,198,789	903,702	487,999	41.1	22.2	54	8,133
Greece	11	225,206	99,541	39,816	44.2	17.7	40	3,620
France	61	2,126,630	980,376	519,599	46.1	24.4	53	8,518
Belgium	10	370,824	156,859	79,998	42.3	21.6	51	8,000
Germany	82	2,794,926	872,017	715,054	31.2	25.6	82	8,720
USA	296	12,416,505	2,632,299	1,601,729	21.2	12.9	61	5411
Global	6,438	44,665,437	12,595,653	5,538,514	28.2	12.4	44	860

Source: World Bank 2007b: 194–6, 226–32.

the law mean that the state obtains little revenue from those who should be making the largest payments. Lack of efficient mechanisms for investigating profits and the wealth of individuals and companies, together with the influence exerted by business upon officials and the media, has also afforded protection to tax evaders. In effect there has been an inverted pyramid of taxation, with the middle class paying most direct revenue because its income is readily taxed through public institutions or through small enterprises where the state can easily intervene to deduct revenue. Until 2004 individuals earning less than E£50,000 paid 20 per cent in tax; those earning more than E£50,000 paid at a 32 per cent rate. Under the government of Prime Minister Ahmed Nazif, a new law raised the limit of tax exemption to E£9,000 a year. Between this level and incomes of E£20,000 a year, tax was set at 10 per cent; between E£20,000 and E£40,000 it reached 15 per cent; for incomes above E£40,000, whether for individuals, small businesses or corporations, the tax level was set at 20 per cent. The law exempted all savings, stocks and bonds from taxes, and cancelled exemptions and tax breaks granted to foreign direct investments (FDI).

Considering the rising cost of living, an increased basic level for exemption was a positive development, while excluding savings was a necessary step to enhance savings levels, which had been at low levels compared to the global average and to the average recorded in developing countries. So, too, with cancellation of exemptions for FDI, since exemption did not play a role in enhancing foreign investment, as companies had to pay taxes in their country of origin. Exemption of the profits of stocks and bonds from any sort of taxation, however, had the effect of encouraging 'hot money' transactions in the stock exchange – speculation by those intent on making exceptional profits and who have long been uninterested in the stability of the economy. This measure served the interests of a wide sector of the upper class, notably that with roots in the illicit economy and that is driven by the 'hit-and-run' culture of instant profits. Even worse was the creation of a new tax band for all those whose trade and industrial profits exceed E£40,000 a year. Here the new law equated the tax burden on small investors and owners of small and micro-enterprises with that to be paid by mega-capitalists whose profits might reach tens, hundreds or thousands of millions of pounds every year. This demonstrated a vulgar bias towards the upper class; it also lacked the minimum consideration of fairness evident in most states, which demand higher tax from those with higher incomes on the basis that they benefit disproportionately from public expenditure on infrastructure and services.

Competition and monopoly laws: weak legislation, weaker implementation

The anti-monopoly law introduced in 2004 had long been impeded by those with an interest in preventing any such legislation. In its final form it did little to inhibit monopoly or protect those subject to manipulation by the large producers. The law set a limit of 35 per cent of the total volume of production of a commodity in the market (this is a relatively high ceiling to start with and at best legalises oligopolies). At this level market share would not be considered harmful and would not be subject to prosecution – as long as the government deemed that the producer involved was not abusing its position to harm the interests of consumers or competitors. The law excluded the transport and communications sectors, claiming that they were already closely monitored and supervised by the government.

The anti-monopoly and competition protection agency, the Egyptian Competition Authority (ECA), should have been autonomous and free of political influence. In fact it is nothing more than a fact-finding and monitoring entity affiliated to the executive authority of the state. Under the new law, prosecutions cannot be initiated unless there is a written request from a minister or an official delegated by him/her; those directly affected by monopoly are not permitted to intervene. The law also stipulates that when a minister or official has initiated prosecution the two parties must opt for reconciliation before a court verdict is issued. Fines to be imposed on the offender range from E£30,000 to E£10 million – sums which are no deterrent to monopolists such as those in the cement or steel sectors, who make hundreds of millions of pounds in profit. In a further evasion, the law does not require companies to modify their practices by surrendering a monopoly position through dividing or reallocating their resources.

When the first trials were held under the new law, the ECA reported the operation of a cartel among cement companies, alleging that a group of businesses had conspired to raise prices by means including limiting production. Some companies had seen an explosive rise in profits: during the first six months of 2008 Suez Cement, Egypt's largest cement company, reported a 28.8 per cent increase in profits to E£768 million. In August 2008, twenty executives, including senior officials of Suez Cement, Misr Beni Suef Cement, Misr Qena Cement, Torah Cement and Al-Ameriyah Cement, were found guilty of price-fixing. The judge in the case, Hisham Hamdy, told the court that they had caused 'deliberate harm' and fined each defendant E£10 million, with a further E£10 million for each company. According to a local industry analyst the fines would have little effect, as they were 'insignificant' in relation to the companies' revenues (El-Madany 2008).

During debates on the law, officials had suggested that it should penalise offenders with fines of 10–15 per cent of an offending company's profits. Prominent among those opposing the measure was Ahmed Ezz, the NDP's secretary for organisational affairs and chair of the parliamentary planning and budget committee. Ezz has repeatedly been accused of operating a monopoly in the steel industry by means of his influence in companies closely linked through personal holdings: in 2004 he was one of the main targets of protests by democracy activists who alleged that he used his political status to advance business interests. His Ezz-Dekhela Group controls over 60 per cent of steel rebar production (steel rebar accounts for 80 per cent of all steel sales in Egypt). One independent analysis of the Egyptian sector describes 'a very strong and excessively dominant monopoly power [that of Ezz] ... seven times as strong as its next best challenger' (Selim 2006: 87). In 2008 a public prosecutor requested investigation of dealings in which Ezz had moved shares between his major companies, allegedly causing heavy losses to the government.[1] Ezz denies operating a cartel but has noted that problems arise when entrepreneurs play leading roles in national politics, commenting cryptically that Egypt 'lack[s] the procedures that separate public work and private interests' (Elyan and Salah-Ahmed 2008).

Tariffs: serving importers, not consumers

The current regime's policy on customs tariffs has been a defining feature of its economic policy. In 2004 the average tax imposed on imports was reduced to 9 per cent. The system was also simplified, cutting the number of taxable categories from twenty-seven to six. In 2007 a presidential decree announced further changes which aimed 'to make the customs tariff a catalyst for economic prosperity, facilitation and improve the lives of all Egyptians' (Ministry of Finance 2007).

Reform was much needed, said its proponents, to end protectionist policies that had made Egyptian industries globally uncompetitive and allowed them to take advantage of domestic consumers by offering goods of low quality at high prices. When a decision was made to lower these tariffs, however, legislation failed to specify the profit margin for importers by means of coordination between the state's economic administration and the General Union of Chambers of Commerce – a necessary step to ensure that reduction of duties would lead to lower prices on imported goods. This would have moved revenues lost by the state due to the fall in customs duties – amounting to some E£3 billion – to consumers. In fact these revenues moved to the pockets of importers, as the law did not affect market prices. The outcome of reform was to confirm and solidify the influence of traders and of commercial networks, which have long played a key role in supporting the regime.

Employment

Employment policy has led to an enormous increase in joblessness. Before 1984 policy was focused on the state's commitment to hire all graduates of the university system. This was efficient when in the 1950s and 1960s the state was establishing new projects that created real jobs. When this process slowed and then stopped, the effect was to pile up unneeded employees in existing projects or within the state apparatus – to create hidden unemployment. The problem was not in the employment policy itself; rather, it was not complemented by initiatives to create real job opportunities. Successive governments made use of increasing labour migration to states of the Gulf region and to Iraq and Libya, gradually abandoning their commitment to employing graduates without establishing an alternative employment strategy and assuming that other states would continue to absorb an important segment of the Egyptian labour force.

In the 1980s the labour market across the Arab region contracted. In 1986 a fall in oil prices affected many economies, followed by a very sharp decline in employment opportunities in Iraq and Kuwait, both of which had absorbed many Egyptian migrants. The end of the Iran–Iraq war in 1988 released many Iraqi males who had earlier been conscripted; the Iraqi invasion of Kuwait in 1990, followed by an international boycott and then a US-led military offensive, also radically reduced the numbers of jobs available for Egyptians. Unemployment in Egypt has since risen steadily. Government statistics indicate that some 2 million people are jobless: in 2006–07, they suggest, the unemployment rate was 9.1 per cent of a labour force (employed and unemployed) said to amount to 22.1 million people (Egyptian Central Bank 2008: 119). Data from the World Bank, calculated from official documents of the Egyptian state, suggest a different picture. As early as 2002 the net Egyptian labour force comprised 25.9 million people (World Bank 2004: 42). Since the net increase in the labour force (newcomers less those who die or reach the age of retirement) is some 800,000 persons annually, by 2007–08 the total labour force amounted to some 30 million people. Some 2 million Egyptians work abroad and 20.1 million work inside Egypt; the total number of unemployed therefore amounts to 7.9 million and the true unemployment rate is now 26.3 per cent, and, on some estimates, the rate in the 15 to 29 age group is over three times that figure.

Incomes

Those in employment face the problem of an incomes policy that has become a key mechanism for pressuring both the middle class and the working class through continuous erosion of real wages. Despite the introduction in 2004 of a unified labour law, establishing a Higher Council for Wages charged with the calculation of a national minimum wage, the Council has failed to set a wage proportional to the growing cost of living; meanwhile wage levels have fallen sharply as productivity has increased. Between 1980 and 1984 the average annual pay of workers in the industrial sector was $2,210, while the added value of each worker was $3,691. Between 1995 and 1999 average pay for the sector decreased to $1,863 annually, while added value for each worker increased to $5,976 (World Bank 2006a: 66). This example is consistent with a general intensification of income inequality and a fall in living standards for the mass of people.

Increased prices for basic goods have brought further problems and deterioration of living standards for most Egyptians. Wage increases have not matched inflation and purchasing capacity has declined sharply. In 1970 the monthly salary of a new university graduate appointed by the government could buy 68 kg of meat monthly – beef is the main source of animal protein in Egyptian cuisine. In 1977 the salary was increased to E£28 monthly, enough to buy 35 kg of meat at prevailing prices. Finally, in 2008 the salary of a new government employee increased to E£210 monthly, enough to buy 6 kilos of meat (for more details, see El-Naggar 2005b).

This decline in potential consumption of a basic component in mainstream Egyptian diets – and, more generally, the fall in purchasing power of many Egyptians – is only one example of deteriorating living standards. The real income of a university graduate joining the state apparatus has deteriorated precipitately, pushing state employees who do not have other sources of income into a deep hole of poverty. Leading state officials and technocrats inside the government meanwhile receive incomes which include commissions, incentives and incidental expenses of legendary proportions, often reaching tens of thousands of pounds a month.

National economic performance

Among the most widely used indicators of economic performance are those which measure overall growth, inflation and domestic debt. Growth in GDP in Egypt over the past twenty-five years has been the lowest since the 1950s. During that decade growth averaged 6 per cent; in the early 1960s it peaked at 8.3 per cent (Zaki 1985: 242). Between 1965 and 1980 average growth was 6.8 per cent, and average annual growth from 1950 to 1980 was also some 6.8 per cent (World Bank 1990: 212). Figures from elsewhere in the Global South demonstrate that such rates compared well with those for many other states: between 1965 and 1980 average growth of GDP in China was 6.4 per cent, in India 3.6 per cent, in Thailand 7.2 per cent, in Malaysia 7.3 per cent, and in South Korea 9.6 per cent (World Bank 1990: 212). Moreover, from the early 1950s to the mid-1970s growth was supported mainly by funds generated within Egypt. At the end of the October war of 1973 total external debt (in addition to military debts to the Soviet

Union, which were eventually cancelled) was US$2.7 billion (Zaki 1985: 147). Due to the shift in economic policy associated with *infitah* and to greatly accelerated foreign borrowing, within a few years external debt had been multiplied many times – by 1980 it stood at US$21 billion (World Bank 1995: 20).

For twenty-five years from the early 1980s annual growth of GDP was relatively modest. Between 1983 and 2007 it averaged 4.3 per cent (based on IMF data from official Egyptian statistics). In comparison, the growth rate in China was 10 per cent, in India 6.2 per cent, and in Malaysia, South Korea and Thailand some 6 per cent (IMF 1990, 2007). In the 1960s Egypt had been an economic leader in the developing world; thirty years later it was in the ranks of the underachievers.

The last twenty-five years have seen the highest inflation in modern Egyptian history. According to the IMF (1990), between 1960 and 1970 annual inflation was 2.9 per cent; between 1971 and 1981 it increased to 9.5 per cent. During the first ten years of Mubarak's rule, from 1982 to 1991, it reached 18.3 per cent (El-Naggar 2005a). Though inflation declined in the second half of the 1990s, by 2004 it was again increasing, reaching over 20 per cent in June 2008 according to some reports.[2] The official figure for the past 25 years is an annual rate of 12 per cent – still the highest in recent history and one which subverts investment and increases income inequality, as salaried state employees and waged workers are disadvantaged in relation to those able to profit from speculative activity.

As we have seen, there has been a startling increase in external debt – although this does not match the current dangerous level of domestic debt – created to compensate for a budget deficit now equal to some 10 per cent of GDP. According to the Central Bank of Egypt, in 2006–07 internal debt reached E£651 billion, a threefold increase on the level reached in 1999 and a figure equal to 89 per cent of GDP (Egyptian Central Bank 2008). This means that internal debt in relation to total national production has exceeded all the usual safety limits.

Tyranny of corruption

Corruption is widespread, as can be seen in the allocation of contracts by the state for commodities, equipment and construction projects, and in the licensing of economic enterprises. This has been complemented by a long series of illicit dealings during privatisation of the public sector.

Supporters of privatisation claim that it is a solution to deteriorating economic performance and corruption in the state sector and that it is now under way worldwide, so that Egypt cannot buck a global trend. Opponents insist that it has been imposed on indebted countries by international financial powers for the latter's benefit, and that wide implementation does not mean that it is the right solution in Egyptian circumstances – or indeed in developing countries in general. Privatisation has nonetheless gone ahead, involving some of the most advanced public-sector companies and accompanied by high levels of corruption in which assets have been sold at levels which massively undervalue companies involved. Three examples demonstrate the scale of abuse:

1. In 1994 the state sold the Egyptian Bottling Company to the private sector. The American accountancy giant Cooper & Lybrand had evaluated its assets in 1993, calculating them at E£76 million. The advisory office of the Holding Company for Food Industries re-evaluated them, estimating the highest market value as E£140 million. In 1994 Egyptian Bottling was sold to a consortium of investors for E£157.6, the contract stipulating that buyers would invest E£180 million during the following five years. In 1999 Pepsi-Cola International bought 77 per cent of the company from the new owners for E£1,340 million (*Al-Ahram*, 5 February 1999). Hence, the total value of the company at this time was some E£1,740 million – more than eleven times the price of its sale in 1994, which indicates that the assets had been grossly miscalculated, so that the new owners had been able to make massive profits from their sale to Pepsi.

2. In 1994 the state also sold El Nasr Boilers Company in another landmark deal. El Nasr occupied a large site at Manial Shiha near Cairo – a key zone for property development. Until 1991, when Minister of Public Enterprises Atef Ebeid ordered a restructuring, it had been profitable. The company soon recorded losses amid allegations that the ministerial order had been a deliberate attempt to change the company's economic performance and justify a sale to the private sector. The task of evaluating the company for

privatisation was allocated to the American Bechtel corporation, which produced an estimate of US$16–24 million (note the huge range), less even than the land occupied by El Nasr, which at 1994 prices was worth US$100 million (see El-Naggar 2005b). Despite protests from the company's workers, privatisation went ahead: in December 1994 it was sold to the US–Canadian group Babcock & Wilcox. After deduction of debts and taxes owed by the company the sale price was a mere E£2.5 million – less than US$750,000. This deal was chosen despite the fact that another bidder had offered an extra US$10 million, plus a commitment to pay the company's debts and taxes.

3. Privatisation of the Egyptian American Bank (EAB) in 2005–06 involved one of the Egypt's most effective financial institutions. In 2005 EAB profits had been E£337 million; the week before its sale shares on the Cairo stock exchange were worth E£56 each. When shortly the bank was sold to the French institution Calyon for just E£45 a share it was also agreed that the new owners would hold the profits of the previous year, E£5 per share, so that the real selling price was a mere E£40 per share. Small investors, who held 28.2 per cent of the shares, lost heavily, while the state lost some E£320 million.

The case of EAB illustrates the unholy marriage between the state and business that is characteristic of the current regime. Two ministers with Cabinet rank – Ahmad al-Maghraby, minister of housing, and Mohamed Mansour, minister of transport – have bought the institution, in association with Calyon. The two Egyptians own 25 per cent, with the rest held by the French company. Under the law it is mandatory to call an extraordinary general meeting of such an institution to approve a sale. This did not take place – a clear violation which demonstrates the extent of business influence at the heart of the regime.

In 2008 the Corruption Perceptions Index produced by Transparency International ranked Egypt at 115 out of 180 states, noting that its overall score had worsened in relation to the previous year (Carr 2008). According to the World Bank (2008), Egypt stands alongside states such as Mauretania, Mozambique and Mongolia in failing to control corruption. In the Middle East, Egypt is ranked 13 out of 18 states, above only Libya, Iran, Yemen, Syria and Iraq. In 2005 the NDP declared that it was ready to tackle the problem. Addressing the party's annual conference, Minister of Investment Mahmoud Mohiedden said: 'We admit that corruption is an issue and that it has to be addressed... We want to be frank about the problem. We also want to be frank about how we are dealing with it', announcing that the party was in the process of drafting 'a comprehensive programme to eliminate corruption' (IRIN 2006). Others suggest, however, that corruption is part of the relationship between business and the state. In 2006 the Kifaya movement produced a 249-page report, *Corruption in Egypt*, detailing alleged malpractice in the privatisation programme and in the ministries of health, agriculture, petroleum, finance and antiquities (see Chapter 1). Nabil Abdel-Fattah of the Al-Ahram Center for Strategic Studies observes that anti-corruption measures have proved ineffective, 'with the result that corruption has become a system of law in Egypt organising relations between citizens and public officials, and between workers and employers in the private sector' (Carr 2008).

'Hot' money

In the 1990s regime officials talked of making Egypt a 'Tiger on the Nile' – a representative in the Middle East of the 'Tiger' economies then making an impact in South and East Asia. The term became a catchphrase, used repeatedly by business people, economists and journalists. In 2004 the US ambassador to Egypt, David Welch, declared that Egypt was in transformation; what was required to complete the process was will on the part of local businessmen and their associates abroad. He told a meeting of the American Chamber of Commerce in Egypt: 'You know what you have to do ... Just do it, and you'll truly see a tiger on the Nile' (AmCham 2004). Egypt is not progressing towards Tiger status, however. Economic changes such as those associated with China, South Korea and the newly industrialising countries (NICs) of the 1970s and 1980s are not in evidence. The government's industrial strategy proposes rapid growth in medium- and high-tech industry with the aim of making Egypt a 'pioneer exporter' in the Middle East and North Africa of consumer electronics, automotive components and biotechnology (Wahish 2006).

But a fraction of Egyptian exports are destined for the Middle East
– in 2006–07 only 12.4 per cent of total exports reached states of the
region, including North Africa (Central Bank of Egypt 2008). The
main destinations for Egyptian products were the European Union
and the United States, which in 2006–07 received over 60 per cent
of total exports, the bulk consisting of petroleum products, textiles
and agricultural goods (Central Bank of Egypt 2008). Rather than
consolidation of major new production sectors, as in the case of the
Tigers (and more recently the 'Dragon' economies such as Indonesia
and Thailand) Egypt has witnessed hesitant and uneven growth, while
traditional core industries, notably textiles, have retreated.

Overall growth has been associated with large foreign investments
in tourism and in construction, which grew 16 per cent in 2006–07,
prompting the *Financial Times* (2007) to warn of 'bubble fears'. As
returns on property have boomed, money has surged in from abroad:
by 2007 a third of investment in Egyptian equities, notably in real
estate, was held by overseas investors (*Financial Times* 2007). During
a few months in 2008 the Cairo stock market lost almost 40 per
cent of its value as investors became more fearful of rising inflation
(then at a twenty-year high) and of general economic instability
(El-Madany 2008). Speculative money began to depart as quickly
as it had arrived: when in September 2008 stock markets worldwide
collapsed, there was a further run on the Cairo exchange – part of
what one local trader called 'retail panic' (El-Madany 2008). Rather
than producing a resilient Tiger with a broader industrial base and
an effective export agenda, Mubarak's embrace of deregulation and
'hot' money has increased instability and the problem of very rapid
speculative movements exaggerated by volatility of commodity prices.
By September 2008 food prices in urban areas had risen over 30 per
cent over the previous twelve months (Shahine 2008).

Conclusion

Economic policies of the past twenty-five years have aimed at decreasing the role of the state in industry and commerce and strengthening
the role of private capital. This is consistent not only with neoliberal
policy in general but with changes in the structure of the ruling class
in Egypt, which has moved away from the state capitalist model to

embrace a system in which bureaucrats and private businessmen work together in nepotistic networks that accumulate enormous wealth for those involved.

True levels of poverty and social marginalisation in Egypt are not reflected in official statistics, which are routinely manipulated to present an inaccurate picture of the distribution of wealth – as indicated by the different estimates provided by Egyptian government institutions (such as the Center for Information and Decision Making Support, the Egyptian Agency for Statistics, and various ministries) and by international financial institutions. Independent analysis shows that inequalities are becoming much more pronounced. In the late 1980s owners of property assets accounted for 51.5 per cent of the annual GDP; by the mid-1990s their share had reached 71.4 per cent, and by 2007 it was 80 per cent (Al-Ahram 2006, 2008). The share acquired by wage-earners decreased from 48.5 per cent of GDP in the late 1980s to 28.6 per cent in 1995 and less than 20 per cent in 2007 (Al-Ahram 2008). Today more than 95 per cent of Egypt's 5.8 million state employees and their families are considered to be poor even by World Bank standards (living under $2 a day per person) or to be extremely poor (living under $1 a day per person). Using data from a survey carried out in 1999–2000, the Bank suggests that the poorest 10 per cent of the Egyptian population received 3.7 per cent of income, while the poorest quintile (20 per cent) received 8.6 per cent of income. The second quintile received 12.1 per cent of income; the third quintile received 15.4 per cent of income; the fourth quintile received 20.4 per cent of income; while the top quintile received 43.6 per cent of income. Meanwhile the wealthiest 10 per cent of the population received 29.5 per cent of the nation's income. Yet these data, which the World Bank received from the Egyptian government, do not include the huge incomes acquired through corruption and theft of public money, nor that generated in the illicit economy through trading in antiquities, drugs, currency, weapons and prostitution.

Egypt has all manner of resources for development. The problems of corruption and mismanagement have nonetheless led to poor performance under successive administrations and to severe deterioration of the country's international status. During the Nasserist era Egypt was indeed a 'Tiger' and a leading regional power, providing a model for many countries. It then became an arena for corruption that rendered useless much of its development potential. Radical changes are now required in the political and socio-economic system so that the country can achieve its potential and live up to its economic heritage.

3

The land and the people

Ray Bush

In March 2005 armed men laid siege to the hamlet of Sarandu in the Nile Delta. They drove away men of the village and began destroying crops, attacking women and children who resisted. When people arrived from surrounding settlements, the armed group – associated with a local landlord – eventually fled, but police soon arrived and began arresting villagers. Testimonies taken by human rights organisations describe police breaking into homes, stealing food and valuables, and beating women who attempted to protect husbands and sons. Fifty people were arrested, including at least thirteen women and five children under the age of 10. For several weeks police continued night-time raids on Sarandu, seizing women and young children: one woman is known to have died following a severe beating (Human Rights Watch 2005a).[1]

The events are typical of conflicts across Egypt following implementation of a law permitting landowning families from the colonial era to 'reclaim' their properties. Invariably the police back landowners against the fellahin,[2] supporting a policy integral to the government's policy for rural change. The stakes are high: Salah Nawar, the landlord involved in Sarandu, reflects the view of many state officials that each battle is a defence of newly restored landed interests. 'If the peasants get away with this, such things will spread all over', he suggests. 'They [the fellahin] will revolt and attack all the owners' (Williams 2005b). This chapter examines the context for such conflicts. It considers continuity and change in rural Egypt since the time of Nasser, raising questions about the persistence of small farmers and the government's strategy to reward large landholders. It suggests that events like those in Sarandu are the outcome of a policy that has already produced a subordinated agrarian capitalism which has much in common with Egypt of the colonial era.

Egypt's agricultural sector employs more than 30 per cent of the country's labour force and accounts for about 17 per cent of GDP (World Bank 2005). The fertile soil of the Nile Valley and the Delta is mostly double cropped yet Egypt is a food deficit country, importing 40 per cent of its food needs (World Bank 2001a). Farming is dominated by smallholders who farm less than one feddan each (0.4 hectare); more than 75 per cent of farmers hold only 50 per cent of the total farm area (Government of Egypt 2000). Since 1987 agrarian strategy has centred on marginalising these small peasants and attacking their standards of living. Law 96 of 1992 revoked Nasser's legislation of the early 1950s, which had given tenants rights in perpetuity. Nasser's reforms for the first time provided a strategy of rural development that restrained the power of Egypt's historically strong pasha class. The current regime appears to be committed to a long-term policy of repression, preventing rural resistance to economic reform and, under the new law, pursuing what amounts to a national land grab.

Nasser and agrarian reform

At the heart of the strategy introduced by the Free Officers in July 1952 was a desire to modernise Egypt. The Officers had inherited a stagnant economy – the average Egyptian was worse off in 1950 than in 1910 (Yapp 1996: 62). One mechanism to promote growth and poverty reduction was to redistribute land. At the time of the revolution 20 per cent of cultivated land was owned by 0.1 per cent of landowners (El Ghonemy 1990). These owners inherited land distributed by the nineteenth-century ruler Mohamed Ali to clients who were part of his new apparatus of state (Cuno 1992). In 1952, 3 million fellahin owned less than one feddan. The near-landless represented 75 per cent of landowners but only held 13 per cent of cultivable land (King 1977). These poor rural dwellers rebelled at various times in the early twentieth century, opposing the luxurious lifestyles of absentee landlords. As one commentator noted, 'The pre-1952 land based power structures obstructed rural development and stratified the rural society into an upper class minority of rich landlords and cotton merchants and a mass of very low income and poor fellahin' (El-Ghonemy 1990: 226–7).

Nasser's land reforms of 1952 and 1961 aimed to distribute land to the landless and near-landless, to improve incomes and to raise agricultural production. Estates of the royal family were seized and foreign ownership banned. Rents were reduced to seven times the land tax (set according to location and fertility and revised every ten years) and limitations were imposed on the size of landholdings. An upper limit for individual ownership was set at 300 feddans in 1952 and 100 feddans in 1961. There were further reforms in 1963 and 1969 limiting individual ownership to 50 feddans. Nasser wanted the reforms to shift power away from large landowners; at the same time he wished to raise surplus production in the countryside and drain it towards urban expansion and the industrial sector (Radwan and Lee 1986). The strategy aimed to expand the area of irrigated land, to increase efficiency of production and improve marketing structures. It was based upon establishment of legal rights for tenants and minimum wages for agricultural labourers.

Nasser's land reforms were the most extensive in the Middle East. The Land Reform Act stated that they were intended 'to build Egyptian Society on a new basis by providing free life and dignity to each peasant and by abolishing the wide gap between classes and by removing an important cause of social and political instability'.[3] Private property was retained and family farms continued, so that as little as one-seventh of cultivable land was taken from large landowners and distributed to smallholders; Egypt was nonetheless the only country in the region to pass land from the state to the peasant farmer. Those with five feddans or less made some gains. In 1952 they had represented 94 per cent of owners, controlling 35 per cent of the cultivated area. After the first reforms they owned 52 per cent of cultivated land. Middle peasants, those with 11 to 50 feddans, gained the most: after the reforms they accounted for 3 per cent of all landowners, owning 24 per cent of the cultivated area (Abdel-Fadil 1975).

Nasser's reforms have been criticised for not redistributing more land: by 1980 only 13.9 per cent of cultivated land had been redistributed to 9.6 per cent of agricultural households (El-Ghonemy 1990). They have also been criticised for providing compensation and allowing families to retain land holdings. The significance of the reforms exceeds the size of distributed land, however. They helped to reduce poverty and to promote economic growth. The economy benefited from increased external labour migration and increased state food and farming subsidies, boosting agricultural production, as did improvements in the supply of rural credit (El-Ghonemy 1993, 1999).

Some of the contradictions in Nasser's nationalist populism are evident in this policy and its outcomes. His agrarian strategy generated support from a peasantry he also tried to subdue – part of an approach in which he sought to obtain political compliance in exchange for improving living standards for the mass of Egyptians (Waterbury 1983; Mansfield 1969; Hinnebusch 1990). Gross domestic product doubled between 1961 and 1970; economic growth was about 7 per cent between 1955 and 1965; and per capita income grew at a more modest 2 per cent as population growth stripped away higher gains. The period 1955 to 1965 also witnessed high rates of investment, averaging 17 per cent of GDP (Stephens 1971). Debt accompanied growth, however, as ambitious plans for development took their toll. The biggest blow to Nasser came in the 1967 war with Israel. Military defeat and the attempt at reconstruction that followed took a heavy financial toll. Israel's occupation of Sinai destroyed oil revenues and Suez Canal rents, and arms spending increased 600 per cent between 1967 and 1973. Nasser moved towards a programme of economic 'liberalisation', which was rapidly accelerated after his death in 1970, and which was to have profound implications for rural society as a whole.

'De-Nasserisation'

After the 1973 war with Israel Anwar Sadat initiated the *infitah*, or 'opening', often called the 'Open Door' policy. At the core of his reforms was the idea of attracting foreign investment and Western technology, and encouraging Egyptian private capital. Buoyed by the liberation of Sinai and his increased political legitimacy, Sadat allied himself with conservative state officials and landed elite interests, promoting de-sequestration of land nationalised under Nasser. After 1975 he called for an end to the freeze on rents enforced since 1952, stepping up his attack on the landless and near-landless and limiting activities of the agrarian reform co-operatives whose membership had been elected by peasant farmers (Springborg 1990).

The old landlord class greeted these changes enthusiastically and was soon on the offensive against the peasantry and those associated with earlier land reforms. Many large landlords had survived two decades of change in the countryside, maintaining important lobby groups within the apparatus of state – notably in the Ministry of Agriculture and the Agronomists' Union – and in parliament, where they had strong representation on the Agricultural Affairs Committee. During the early 1970s the committee had exploited Nasser's relaxation of some state controls, winning rent increases, watering down laws on security of tenure, and successfully opposing taxes on horticultural products. As *infitah* progressed, benefiting mainly commercial interests, the agrarian bourgeoisie consolidated its position. Representatives of many landowning families entered Sadat's reshaped parliament as independent deputies, re-establishing an effective national lobby for traditional interests. Sadat accommodated some of their most important demands, notably by agreeing that reclaimed land would not be subject to the existing ownership limit of 50 feddans – a means of enabling those affected by the 1952 law to re-establish their estates. As the pace of change accelerated, foreign companies were allowed to lease large areas of farmland to be run on corporate lines. The first investment came from Coca-Cola, creating an important bridgehead for agribusiness (Hinnebusch 1985: 143). In 1979 the private agrarian lobby achieved a further breakthrough, securing compensation for landowners expropriated under the last of Nasser's reforms.

Sadat's reforming zeal was helped initially by high oil prices and by migrant remittances from the Gulf and other Arab countries. Remittances reached an average of $3 billion of annual flows to Egypt in the mid-1970s, but while the regime began with the rhetoric of promised economic growth its policies floundered in high levels of external debt (Ibrahim and Löfgren 1996). Corruption became widespread, while the mass of Egyptians experienced increasingly high levels of poverty. Dissatisfaction mounted, with bread riots in January 1977 protesting cuts in food subsidies: *infitah* limped along until in 1981 Sadat was assassinated. He had not provided a working alternative to Nasser's statist formulas and Mubarak inherited an economic crisis which by the mid-1980s was having a severe impact in the countryside, where there was net return migration and increasing unemployment.

By 1974 Egypt was the world's third highest importer of grain. During the 1970s imports had quadrupled to fill a gap between wheat production, which was growing at less than 2 per cent per annum, and consumption, which was increasing at 9 per cent (Mitchell 1995). There was an eightfold increase in per capita imports of food grains and the agricultural trade balance fell from a surplus of $300 million in 1970 to a deficit of $800 million in 1977. By the mid-1980s the agricultural trade deficit was $2.5 billion (USAID and Government of Egypt 1995). Income that may have been generated as a result of *infitah* was seldom invested locally in industrial or agricultural production – between 1980 and 1992 gross investment in agriculture fell from 31 per cent to 23 per cent (El-Ghonemy 1999:12). These problems were part of a deepening economic crisis that led the Mubarak regime to accept an economic reform and structural adjustment programme (ERSAP), finally agreed with international financial institutions in 1991 and stricter than any accepted in earlier negotiations with the IMF (Butter 1992; Bromley and Bush 1994). ERSAP led to reductions in state subsidies, liberalisation of interest rates, restoration of private currency dealing and sales tax, and a reduction in bureaucracy, which was believed to have inhibited expansion of trade. The budget deficit was cut, along with Egypt's official government and military debt, which was reduced by the Paris Club of creditors by about $28 billion (Bush 1999).

Liberalisation

ERSAP aimed at wholesale liberalisation of the Egyptian economy. Many of its component strategies had been rehearsed in an agricultural liberalisation initiated in the mid-1980s. Since 1986 the Ministry of Agriculture and Land Reclamation had worked closely with American aid officials to promote agricultural reform. Between

1981 and 1992 growth in the sector was about 2 per cent per annum
– 2 per cent less than was thought necessary to sustain economic
growth and 3 per cent less than the government's target (World
Bank 2001a). By the mid-1980s there was a $3 billion net deficit in
agricultural trade, which the ministry and the United States Agency
for International Development (USAID) blamed on excessive state
intervention, said to inhibit agricultural productivity (Nassar 1993).
USAID was central in driving reform by means of a dual strategy
– through an Agricultural Production and Credit Project and the
Agricultural Policy and Reform Programme. The latter focused on
pricing policy, export-led growth and attempts to emulate the American farm model of extensive capital-intensive agriculture. USAID
stressed that the $250 million invested was intended to remove barriers
to private enterprise, creating a liberal, competitive marketing system
and stimulating sustainable agricultural growth.

Advocates of liberalisation hailed their efforts as a success. Between
1980 and 1990 there was an increase in the real value of crop production for twenty-three major crops, and between 1986 and 1992 wheat
production and farm incomes rose. Falls in food subsidies and an
erosion of controls on cropping patterns were heralded as a success
(Faris and Khan 1993; Fletcher 1996). The area under cultivation
increased from 6.2 million to 9 million feddans as a result of land
reclamation and 'new lands' development. Between 1982 and 1998 cereal
production rose from 8.5 million to 18 million tonnes and vegetable
production from 8 million to 15.2 million tonnes (Government of
Egypt 2005: 5). Yet early declarations of success need to be examined
carefully. Evidence for improvements in rural incomes and changes
to cropping patterns cannot be explained solely by market reforms
or price incentives. It is likely that productivity gains were less the
result of price incentives and more a relaxation of reporting measures:
before 1987 state surveillance made farmers reluctant to divulge what
they actually grew (Mitchell 1999). It is also interesting to note that
early 'successes' have remained a key claim of the government, despite
the fact that the reform process is now more than twenty years old.
It might be expected that evidence for sustained change would be
found in more recent figures, but these do not suggest continued
success in productivity, cropping patterns and exports. Growth in
the agricultural sector has not met expectations of the government

or of USAID: the rate of growth after 1990 was less than for the period 1980 to 1987, and recent failures to boost productivity have led USAID and the World Bank to renew calls for Egypt to embrace a strategy of export-driven growth for horticultural products (World Bank 2001a, 2001b).

Tenure reform

Over the past twenty years neoliberal orthodoxy has converted a state-led redistributive land reform into a market-led agrarian reform (Lahiff et al. 2007). The key mechanism – apart from initiatives linked to pricing, cropping and attempts to favour export crops – has been a frontal assault on the land reform of 1952.

Legal rights for tenants introduced by the Free Officers in 1952 were abruptly severed by Mubarak's Law 96 of 1992. The ruling NDP managed to achieve two significant aims: demonstrating to the international community its serious intent to 'modernise' tenure, and providing enhanced security for landowners, a social class closely aligned to Mubarak's party. Although there was to be a five-year transition period, making the legislation effective from October 1997, rents increased immediately, paving the way for radical redistribution of tenancies and for dispossession of peasant families, especially of female-headed households.

Law 96 was not intended to apply to agrarian reform land or to *awqaf* (religiously endowed land) but soon became a matter of concern throughout the countryside. After 1992 rents increased from seven times the land tax to least twenty-two times the tax. After 1997 landowners could retake 'their' land and charge tenants a market-based rent, so that rents increased by as much as 400 per cent. Many peasants assumed that the regime would be unable to go ahead with the changes: in the words of an old man from a Delta village, 'We simply could not imagine that water would flow upriver' (El-Gawhary 1997). Many were unaware of the detail of the reform until landlords, accompanied by the security forces, visited villages to inform farmers that rents were about to rise and/or that their tenure had ended. Under the new act, tenancies were renewable annually, though written agreements were seldom available. Landlord power increased dramatically: landowners were able to dispose of tenancies at will and many refused to renew contracts, especially in the case of female-headed tenant households and even where women were successful farmers, had agreed to new rents (albeit reluctantly) and had no record of default.

'Lazy' fellahin

The consequences of de-sequestration have been explored by a number of authors (Bush 2002; Saad 2002). Several themes emerge: the politicisation of land promoted by the 1992 Act and its place in the neoliberal rhetoric of the NDP; the failure to raise productivity; the consequences for social differentiation in the countryside; the promotion of subordinate agrarian capitalism; and the level of resistance engendered in rural communities.

Law 96 created an environment in which Egypt's smallholding farmers, tenants and landless were ridiculed by much of the media. The country's press took its lead from parliamentary debates that caricatured fellahin as lazy, wealthy and as continuing beneficiaries of a Nasserist revolution irrelevant to modern Egypt (Saad 2002: 104, 109; Saad 1999). For the government-controlled press the peasantry had become parasitic upon national society in general and the landowners in particular:

> Tenant farmers were portrayed as 'lazy peasants watching videos and abandoning the land to travel abroad abroad to buy more consumer goods'. It was claimed that 'tenant's [sic] pockets were filling with tens of thousands of pounds... buying 70, 80 feddans of land from their former owners and driving around in Mercedes and Peugeot cars', great status symbols in the countryside. (Saad quoted in Tingay 2004: 22)

By contrast, landowners were 'needy yet respectable middle-class helpless citizens oppressed by merciless tyrants' (Saad quoted in Tingay 2004: 22).

These references recall earlier attacks on the peasantry at a time when the state was attempting to advance the interests of private capital. During the mid-1970s, with national economic and political agendas set by Sadat's *infitah*, the landlord lobby in parliament had undertaken a similar offensive. Ansari (1987: 181) comments that its members were in a 'vengeful' mood, blaming fellahin for all manner of ills and scapegoating those who supported tenants' interests. In a key debate on agrarian relations, members of parliament railed against the peasantry:

> Speaker after speaker detailed landlord grievances against peasants: they were rebellious and needed no government protection; they lived in luxury while the landowners went hungry; the peasant who was once oppressed had become the oppressor... Without suffering contradiction, the landlords claimed that the peasants profited LE100 per feddan per year while the owner received only LE20 in rent. (Hinnebusch 1985: 177)

Such was hostility against the fellahin that – in an assembly which by law should have been 50 per cent peasant in composition – no peasant representative 'dared raise their voice in defence of their class' (Hinnebusch 1985: 177). The assembly voted overwhelmingly to change agrarian relations law by raising the rent burden on tenants and reducing security of tenure.

Recent ideological offensives on the peasantry conceal real retreats enforced upon tenants by combined efforts of the regime and the landowning class. Figures available since 2000 demonstrate that among the fellahin the most disadvantaged have been further marginalised by Sadat's accommodation of landed interests and by Mubarak's reform. During the 1990s the number of 'fully owned' farmers increased from 1.9 million to 3.2 million, while the number of fully cash-paid rental farmers fell from 387,160 (13.3 per cent of landholders) to 189,355 (5.1 per cent of landholders) in 2000 (Government of Egypt 1990, 2000). Meanwhile changes in the pattern of landholding showed a shift towards larger owners and an increase in the absolute and relative numbers of landless peasants (Bush 2007).

There has been no co-ordinated national response to the new law. Those affected have faced a number of difficulties, including the complex nature of landholding agreements and problems in determining appropriate targets for opposition to the legislation. Fellahin often farm small pieces of land that have been inherited; at the same time they may cultivate tenanted land and engage in sharecropping. This 'tenancy web' (Abdel Aal 2003) has complicated efforts to identify local beneficiaries of the 1992 Act. As Tingay (2004) shows, tenants have often been reluctant to disturb relations with members of the community with whom they must maintain working relationships, and under these circumstances protests have often remained localised and specific.

Resistance to the impacts of Law 96 has been underplayed by the regime, however. This has in part been a function of the posture of denial adopted by political leaders and state officials. In 1997 the minister of agriculture rejected a petition against reform which included 350,000 names, suggesting that popular feeling against government policy could not possibly be so widespread – an arrogance that reflects the approach of urban-based government towards rural challenges to its authority. Two years later a report on land tenure published by USAID and the Ministry of Agriculture claimed that 'good relations' between landlords and tenants meant there had been minimal protest (Tingay 2004: 30). Numerous peasant testimonies and eyewitness accounts from human rights monitors tell a different story. In 1997 the Land Center for Human Rights (LCHR) reported 'violent clashes' in some one hundred villages, with numerous cases of intimidation, illegal detention and torture of villagers by police and other security agencies. According to the LCHR, during the period between 1 September 1997 and 1 May 1998, 17 people died, 533 were wounded and 1,588 were arrested for alleged offences in disputes between landlords and tenants (Land Center for Human Rights 2002).

Because of repression, extensive secret police networks and collusion between landowners and local police, many protests have been covert, unplanned and unorganised: there is nonetheless ample evidence of local resistance. Protests began in 1996 in Bani Suef, south of Cairo, with a demonstration by over 3,000 farmers. In the months that followed there were numerous meetings and petitions, with villagers raising black flags of protest and erecting signs and banners that denounced the law. Groups known as Farmers' Committees for Resistance to Law 96 organised some 200 meetings (Tingay 2004: 32). The regime responded with a campaign of arrests, using a strategy tried and tested over the years against Islamist groups. Resistance continued to spread, however. In July 1997 several thousand tenants gathered in two villages in the southern province of Minya. The crowd set light to houses of local landowners, blocked main roads and set fire to railway tracks and a bus; during an attack by police three people were killed. A day later, tenants in Al Attaf, a village in the Delta, attacked the local office of the agriculture ministry in an attempt to destroy official records: more than 160 people were arrested. In Qamaruna, northeast of Cairo, a 70-year-old farmer and his wife were beaten to death by a landlord and his son after refusing to pay a rent increase (El Gawhary 1997). In the Delta village of Kamshish, a historic centre of peasant resistance, landlords attempted to seize large areas of land: in the face of a strong police presence resistance continued fitfully for several years.

According to the LCHR, as the incremental effects of reform have become clear local resistance has intensified, so that during 2004 there were 49 deaths and 430 arrests in land disputes across the country (Murphy 2005). At the same time landlords have become more confident, applying to the courts for eviction orders they anticipate will be issued routinely. Armed gangs have seized crops and occupied fields by force, sometimes supported by police, with whom many landowners have close relations, including through the ruling NDP. Landlords often blame resistance upon urban political activists, whom they accuse of inflaming feelings at the village level. Salah Nawar, the landowner associated with violence in Sarandu in 2005, alleges just such external interference: 'People come from Cairo and tell them [the peasants] they can have all the land', he says. 'The peasants never acted like this before' (Williams 2005b). He maintains that the rural population is being misled:

> What you have to understand is that the peasants aren't educated; they're very simple and it's been easy for the activists to brainwash them... The activists have lied to them, saying that the land isn't really mine, and have really stirred things up. So I had to call in the police. (Williams 2005b)

Peasants and their supporters maintain that issues of access to the land raise existential questions for the fellahin – that resistance continues to be widespread and that further conflict is inevitable. Fellahin have been reminded of the 'days of the blue gallabeyya' before 1952 when landlords shaped rural life in a seemingly all-encompassing manner. Landlord collusion with security forces, attempts to rig legal rulings on land claims, and attempts to seize land-reform land have all become common practice.

New, new lands

According to the World Bank, the agricultural sector in Egypt has pioneered a reform strategy now applied successfully to the economy as a whole (World Bank 2001a: i). In 2001 it made a celebratory assessment of changes under way since the 1980s:

> Most of the distortions that previously kept the [agricultural] sector from reaching its full potential were lifted during the 1990s. Prices and trading of many inputs and commodities were liberalized, and farmers were allowed to choose their cropping patterns. The agricultural sector is now a fully private sector, operating in a market and export-oriented economy. (World Bank 2001a: i)

The Egyptian government has since repeated the claims, declaring that reform 'has had a positive economic impact at both macro and sectoral levels' (Government of Egypt 2005a: 5). Echoing proposals made by the Bank, state officials argue that Egypt can advance rapidly towards profitable agricultural export activity. In fact since 1999 there have been huge fluctuations in the level of agricultural exports: in the case of cotton, export volume collapsed from 161,000 tonnes to 97,000 tones between 2002 and 2005; while recently agricultural exports as a whole declined – in 2004 they were valued at E£7.6 billion; a year later the figure had fallen to E£6.2 billion (Government of Egypt 2005b). Since 2001 there have been slight increases in exports of potatoes, tomatoes and onions, but improvements have been uneven. Over the longer term the contribution of agriculture to the trade deficit has grown significantly: from 21 per cent in 1974 to 33 per cent in 1998 (El-Din 2000).

Some of these problems have been identified in a frank assessment of Egyptian economic performance produced by the *Financial Times*. The newspaper suggests that overall figures for export growth 'are still desperately low for a country of Egypt's size' (*Financial Times* 2007). It notes that despite progress in some areas, notably oil and gas, in others – especially food – Egypt is becoming more dependent upon imports: 'Egypt still imports nearly all its meat, all its wood, and all its grains, including most of the fava beans used for making *foul*, a staple food.' Close examination of government statistics shows that between 1995 and 2003 there was a fall in areas cultivated for seed cotton, wheat, alfalfa, clover, summer maize, dry beans and dry fenugreek (Government of Egypt 2005b). Land dedicated to intensive production of high-cost fruit, vegetables and flowers for the European market (green beans, new potatoes, strawberries, carnations and medicinal plants have been identified as success stories) consumes water, labour and other inputs, as well as reshaping patterns of cultivation vital to production of staple foods and fodder.

Government officials suggest that, as Egypt is integrated into the world economy, low-income farmers will benefit from the growth process (Government of Egypt 2005a:6). But agrarian policy is not meeting its aims, in part because of continuing lack of interest in smallholders' own ideas about what farmers can offer to an integrated rural development strategy. If the government was serious about rural development it would reveal its commitment by evidence of investment: in fact the budget for 2007 allocated just E£365 million to the sector, amounting to 0.2 per cent of funds dispersed (Al-Gamal 2007). Instead of investing in the activities of smallholders by addressing problems of poverty, low income and uneven access to resources, the government has directed investment to expansion of what are called the 'new, new lands'. These include the New Valley Governorate west of Luxor and the agricultural schemes of Toshka, East Oweinat and North Sinai, which cost some $3.7 billion annually to maintain (Farag 2003).

Toshka is a mega-project: the aim is to create a further 'new valley' parallel to the Nile in the southernmost part of the country by constructing a huge pumping station at Lake Nasser linked to 50 kilometres of main transfer canal, four 22-kilometre side branches and 800 kilometres of feeder pipeline.[4] Completion is scheduled for 2017 at an anticipated cost of $70 billion. Such schemes endorse donor- and IFI-led approaches, with their assumption that boosting exports requires investment in US-style capital-intensive agriculture. They also sustain the myth of Egypt as a 'hydraulic society' in which economic success depends upon projects under the control of a strong central ruler.

Like the foolishness that assumes Egypt can export its way towards a new agricultural nirvana, projects such as Toshka are sucking the life out of the Nile. The strategy is unsustainable. Following increased irrigation run-off at Toshka, which has diminished the flow of the Nile northwards, there have been farmers' protests at the volume and quality of water in the Delta. Critics of the project suggested at the planning stage that Toshka would be unsustainable, but the government ignored calls for systematic environmental impact assessments. The scheme was intended to reduce perceived population pressure from the Delta by employing fellahin to work in Upper Egypt and to drive up exports of fruit and vegetables for European and Gulf dinner tables. These aims have not been met – and in order for the project to continue at all, large incentives have been given to US companies and Saudi investors such as Prince al-Walid bin Talal bin Abdulaziz (Mitchell 2002; *Rural Migration News* 2002; *Trade Arabia* 2007). But even the strongest supporters of agribusiness, such as the American Chamber of Commerce in Egypt (AmCham), admit 'the project has failed to gain steam' (Craig 2008). There is an irony here: the government has declared that its new strategy will be on the basis of 'a limited [state] role… in agricultural development, placing heavy reliance on the private sector and market forces in the production processing and marketing of produce'; at the same time it has reserved a central role for itself in expansion of agriculture outside the Nile Valley and the Delta (Government of Egypt 2005a: 6). For leading politicians and state officials marketisation is embraced as a panacea for problems of the agricultural sector; simultaneously they indicate that there is no private-sector investor willing to invest in the enormous programmes now at the centre of their strategy for agricultural expansion.

Conclusion

The idea that private investment will modernise agriculture has been a mantra of government strategists for many years. In the 1990s USAID argued that private capital would boost export growth (USAID 1992b) but, as we have seen, Egypt has been unable to meet expectations placed on it by IFIs and the rhetoric of its own Ministry of Agriculture and Land Reclamation. Changes in volume and price of agricultural products raise awkward questions about the integrity of the export-led strategy, of which the most important is the fate of Egypt's farmers. The government has responded to suggestions made by the IFIs, USAID and more recently the New Partnership for Africa's Development (NEPAD) by talking about high-value agricultural exports and seeking international aid to back its new schemes. Egypt is unable to deliver: superficially because the strategy is limited to markets to which it has poor access; more fundamentally because there are problems of low volume and poor quality associated with inadequate investment and with the excessive spoils seized by local crony capitalism. The reforms have been poorly implemented and their sequencing has been flawed, notably by liberalising prices and trade before addressing issues of farmers' access to land, inputs and marketing. The most important problem, however, is that reform is part of an agenda for further subordinate incorporation of Egypt into the global food system and for the reward of private property rights rather than social need.

The neoliberal 'post'-Washington Consensus is a strategy to boost international trade that benefits states with existing surpluses in agricultural production; it is not, despite rhetoric to the contrary, of benefit to states such as Egypt. Criticism internationally of this idea intensified during 2008 in the face of mounting of food insecurity in the Global South in general. In Egypt riots at bakeries prompted President Hosni Mubarak to describe price hikes as 'unprecedented' and 'dangerous' and to order the army to bake and distribute subsidised bread (Craig 2008). Bakeries introduced higher-quality bread, sold for 10 piastres, in order to ease demand on 5-piastre loaves. The government intervened with further emergency measures, buying an additional 2.4 million tonnes of wheat and raising prices paid to local farmers to encourage planting. It also instituted a six-month export ban on rice, aiming to compel traders to sell to the local market (Craig 2008). Even AmCham, long an advocate of 'liberal' reform, identifies the link between availability of food, immiseration and social instability, warning of problems to come (Craig 2008).

The issues at stake are not Egypt's integration into the world economy or the prospect that integration will improve national economic performance and food security: Egypt has long been part of a world economy shaped by dominant development agendas. It is likely that the Mubarak regime can continue to extract a strategic rent from the 'international community' for its role in the war against terror, its complicity with specific practices such as 'extraordinary rendition', and as a broker in the Palestinian quest for statehood, providing sufficient revenue to maintain legitimacy and prevent political implosion. But the 'rent card' looks increasingly dog-eared and comes at a cost. Millions of people face the threat of losing their tenuous grip on the land, with the result that local struggles continue, sometimes erupting into battles which involve whole communities.

In 2005, people of the village of Surad, in the Delta province of Gharbiya, refused to return 23 acres of land to landlords who had gained a court decision that they had rights to 'reclaim' their fields. Armed men were sent to the village, leading to a battle in which four people were killed and many wounded. For the lawyer who defended more than fifty villagers arrested by local police the incident was predictable. Landlords had already tried on several occasions to seize the land, he observed, even using the police to accompany them. They had been successfully repelled each time: 'Here', he says, 'people see the land like they see their children: it's precious' (Fathi 2005). As food prices soar, access to the land becomes an increasingly pressing issue – and a guarantee of continued communal struggles.

4

Workers' struggles
under 'socialism' and neoliberalism

Joel Beinin

According to conventional wisdom, the nationalisation of most of Egypt's large-scale industrial, banking, financial, and commercial enterprises in the early 1960s represented the adoption of socialism. By the same token, the policy of *infitah* announced in 1974 is understood to have launched a new economic trajectory embracing a return to capitalist private enterprise, welcoming foreign direct investment, and reorienting the economy away from the Soviet bloc and towards the West. But several factors have remained constant for Egypt's industrial workers over the last half-century. Social relations of production have remained similar: neither under 'socialism' nor under 'capitalism' have blue-collar workers exercised significant influence over conditions in their workplaces, and both public- and private-sector workplaces have been managed in an extremely hierarchical and authoritarian manner, involving considerable implicit and sometimes actual violence (Shehata 2003). Since the establishment of the Egyptian Trade Union Federation (ETUF) in 1957, trade unions have functioned as an arm of the state rather than as democratic representatives of workers, mobilising workers to demonstrate 'popular support' for the divergent policies of successive regimes at the ballot box or in the street.[1] Trade-union elections have always been rigged, with oppositional elements from communists to Muslim Brothers banned from running as candidates for trade-union committees. There have never been direct elections for the executive committees of the twenty-three national general unions or the ETUF executive committee, thus guaranteeing that they remain safely in the hands of regime loyalists.

The state has viewed workers' collective action primarily as a security matter. Despite a court ruling in April 1987 that the right to strike is constitutionally protected and the passage of the Unified Labour Law 12 of 2003, which legalised strikes, there have been no legal strikes in Egypt since Nasser consolidated power in March 1954. Under the 2003 legislation strikes are permitted only under severely restricted circumstances and must have the endorsement, in advance, of the executive committee of the ETUF. In the contested relationship between labour and capital, the latter – whether managed by the state or in the private sector – has been favoured by successive regimes.

Egypt's massive defeat in the 1967 Arab–Israeli War undermined the legitimacy of the Nasser regime and exposed it to significant political and social criticism for the first time since 1954. Its economic policies were in crisis even before the war: the index of real wages peaked in 1964 and fell or remained stagnant until 1972; at the same time the average number of hours worked per week began to rise (Abdel-Fadil 1980; Posusney 1993: 218–19. In 1965 the regime turned to the IMF for assistance in resolving its balance-of-payments crisis; no new social legislation was introduced after that year (Posusney 1993: 219). A retreat from 'socialist' policies was signalled in the 30 March 1968 manifesto, which promoted technocratic solutions to Egypt's economic problems (Cooper 1982).

The 1967 events and consequent diminution of the regime's legitimacy opened a space for working people to express their discontent. In response to declining real wages, the first significant workers' collective actions since 1954 erupted in 1971 and early 1972 in the industrial areas of Helwan (iron and steel workers) and Shubra al-Khayma (textile workers), expressing grievances accumulated during the Nasser era (Beinin 1993). By the second half of 1972, when wages began to rise, strikes and other forms of protest subsided (Posusney 1993: 220). During 1975–76 real wages began to fall again and collective protests resumed (Beinin 1993: 215). The most important action occurred at the Misr Spinning and Weaving Company in the central Delta city of Mahalla al-Kubra – the emblem of Egyptian economic nationalism since it was established by Bank Misr in 1927. A three-day sit-in strike in March 1975 resulted in a wage increase from E£9 to E£15 a day for all public-sector production workers in Egypt.

While this second period of declining wages and labour actions followed the announcement of the Open Door policy, neither the decline in wages nor the strikes it occasioned were caused by the new policy: indeed, it was some ten years before significant changes occurred in the Egyptian economy (Richards 1991: 17–21). The impulse driving the struggles of early 1970s was the secular decline in wages from 1965, which continued until significant numbers of Egyptians began to emigrate to work in the oil-rich Arab countries during the post-1974 oil boom.

Open-door policy

In 1976 Sadat decided to implement the recommendations of an IMF mission that called for dramatic cuts in subsidies on basic consumer commodities (Beinin 1993: 248 – see Chapter 1). This prompted the 'bread riots' of 18–19 January 1977, an intifada that had similarities with urban uprisings against neoliberal policies which later took place in Morocco, Tunisia and Jordan (Beinin 2001: 165–6). This was an immediate response both to IMF-inspired reforms and to longer-term grievances; it had a genuinely national character but at the same time was not a unified movement. Industrial workers initiated the events and played a major role – but this was also one of the first occasions on which Islamists came into the streets promoting their understanding that Egypt's predicament was primarily a moral not a social-economic crisis. The urban crowds of January 1977 were not led by the Left, as the regime claimed, but responded spontaneously to a direct attack on their standard of living.

January 1977 was a victory for the Egyptian popular classes: most importantly, consumer subsidies were restored. But it did not translate into increased militancy, development of independent organisation, or changes in political consciousness of industrial workers or indeed any sectors among the subaltern strata. There is only one recorded instance of a workers' protest in the four years following the 1977 events (Posusney 1993: 222). This suggests that Marsha Pripstein Posusney is correct in characterising the protests of the 1970s and early 1980s as framed by a 'moral economy' consciousness.[2] Popular slogans like 'In the days of defeat, the people could still eat' (raised by strikers in 1975) or 'Nasser always said, "Take care of the workers"' (heard in 1977) suggest that workers were looking back to a period when their wages and, perhaps just as important, their social status were higher than they were in the Sadat era. In the late 1970s the working class was socially and politically disorganised and the continuity of working-class communities disrupted by emigration, while wages began to rise due to sectoral labour shortages. At the same time, both the legal and the illegal left were subjected to repression – a result of Sadat's crackdown following the 1977 events.[3] Consequently, although many public-sector industrial workers were wary of the Open Door economic policy and its implications, there was no broad-based and sustained reaction against it.

Sayyid Habib, a veteran worker at Misr Spinning and Weaving in Mahalla al-Kubra recalled: 'When Sadat announced the Open Door economic policy things were moving forward. The company had 184 clients internationally. Raw materials and labour were cheap. There were around 40,000 workers in the mill.[4] Misr workers appreciated the bonuses Sadat distributed when he visited but he never won their affection as Nasser did. Habib reminisced, 'When Abdel-Nasser died, the female workers wore black. When [the popular singer] 'Abd al-Halim Hafiz died, they also wore black. When Sadat died, no one wore black.'

Intensification of neoliberalism

From 1984, the collapse of the oil boom and increased pressure from international financial institutions to adopt neoliberal policies resulted in price rises and falling real wages (Posusney 1993: 221). In response there was a sharp rise in workers' collective actions (El Shafei 1995). During the mid- and late 1980s some elements of the workers' movement began to assume a political character linked to both the legal and the underground Left. *Al-Ahali*, the newspaper of the legal National Progressive Unionist Party (al-Tagammu'), covered labour issues regularly. Several 'alternative' newspapers and organisations also emerged to give workers a voice outside the framework of the state-dominated trade-union apparatus. Two veteran Marxist textile union activists, the late Taha Sa'd 'Uthman and Mohamed Mutawalli al-Sha'rawi, were among the editors of *Sawt al-'Amil* (Workers' Voice), which began publication in 1985 with an editorial line sharply critical of the historic absorption and repression of the labour movement by the Nasserist state. Textile workers at Mahalla al-Kubra formed the core of an area-wide organisation, Al-Fagr (Dawn), which had several hundred members and which during the mid-1980s issued a newspaper with the same name. Meanwhile textile workers of Shubra al-Khayma produced a local publication, '*Ummal Shubra al-Khayma* (Shubra al-Khayma Workers).

Reactions to legislation in 1984 which doubled workers' contributions to health and pension plans was especially sharp at the Nasr Automotive Company and the Alexandria Transport Authority, forcing the government to withdraw the law and reissue it a few months later with a staggered implementation plan. Nonetheless, there were extremely sharp reactions among textile workers of Alexandria and Kafr al-Dawwar when the new rules were applied: in Kafr al-Dawwar there was a three-day urban insurrection, during which workers and urban crowds cut telephone lines, started fires, blocked transportation and destroyed train carriages before a massive crackdown by security forces restored order. Private-sector workers also joined the 1984–89 strike movement, although they were much less prominent than those of the public sector. Collective actions in the private sector usually involved fewer than 1,000 workers and never drew in the people of industrial cities, as occurred in Kafr al-Dawwar. Many private enterprises were now being located in new cities on the periphery of Cairo, where the social fabric creating mutual interests and obligations was still weak. Moreover, there were very few trade unions in the private sector, so even the minimal organisation and representation afforded by ETUF was absent. Often the demands of private-sector workers were for treatment equivalent to those in the public sector. This was their right according to Law 24 of 1972, although employers evaded the legislation.

Some collective actions of the 1984–89 period had an insurgent character, especially those of Kafr al-Dawwar, the ESCO textile mill near Cairo and the train drivers; nonetheless most strikes were framed by a moral economy consciousness. They aimed to restore wages enjoyed earlier, or demanded parity between private- and public-sector workers. The difference in the two periods is that by the second half of the 1980s the oil boom was over, wages were stagnating, prices were rising sharply, and neoliberal policies – such as doubling workers' contributions to health and pension plans – were being implemented more aggressively.

The absence of a political-economic alternative to neoliberalism might partly explain the relatively meagre long-term organisational and political results of the strike wave. Another factor is the policy of the Tagammu'. During the 1990s the organisation lost much of its popular base because it decided to support the Mubarak regime against the Islamist insurgency based in Upper Egypt and the peripheral slums of Cairo and Alexandria (see Chapter 6). Tagammu' chief Rif'at al-Sa'id devised this strategy in the hope that it would create more space for the secular left to manoeuvre on the margin of an authoritarian regime that showed no signs of weakening – a local expression of the retreat of the left and workers' movements internationally and their failure to articulate viable alternatives to neoliberalism. In addition, after the 1989 strikes at the Helwan Iron and Steel Company, the Mubarak regime became less tolerant of labour dissidence – an aspect of its more repressive character in the 1990s (Kienle 2001).

Two sit-in strikes at the Iron and Steel Company in Helwan in July and August 1989 were among the fiercest confrontations between workers and the state in the 1980s and the most important exception to a trend in which long-term institutions and alternative political visions did not emerge from the conflicts of the period (El Shafei 1995: 22–35). One of the leaders, Kamal 'Abbas, was dismissed for participating in an 'illegal' dispute. In 1990 he became a founding member of the Center for Trade Union and Workers' Services (CTUWS), which subsequently established branches in Shubra al-Khayma, Mahalla al-Kubra and the upper Egyptian city of Nag' Hammadi, site of a large public-sector aluminium mill. Another founding member of the CTUWS and an important source of advice and support rooted in extensive historical experience of labour struggles was the late Yusuf Darwish, a veteran communist and labour lawyer who had represented many trade unions in Shubra al-Khayma and Cairo from the 1930s to the 1950s. He had recruited many of their leaders into Tali'at al-'Ummal (Workers' Vanguard), one of three main trends in the communist movement that in 1958 united to form the Communist Party of Egypt. At one point 'Abbas joined Darwish and another veteran communist militant, the late Nabil al-Hilali, in the leadership of the underground People's Socialist Party, a small group that left the Communist Party of Egypt in the 1990s, objecting to its strategy of supporting the Mubarak regime against the Islamists. After this early association with underground Marxist politics, however, 'Abbas and the CTUWS abandoned overt political demands in favour of a focus on bread-and-butter issues.

Crisis in the textile sector

The upsurge of labour militancy in the second half of the 1980s was set in the context of a structural crisis in the textile sector. The proportion of textile workers in the industrial workforce began declining in 1960; the absolute number of textile workers began declining in 1976 (Abdel-Kader 1998: 79). The index of real wages of textile workers fell from 100 in 1986 to 61 in 1994, an even more precipitous decline than the average of industrial workers (Abdel-Kader 1998: 84). This crisis continued into the 1990s and the first decade of the twenty-first century. Due to lack of capital investment and 'overstaffing', estimated at about 30 per cent, textile industry productivity was lower in 1999 than in 1985 and remains lower than in neighbouring countries such as Tunisia and Turkey. Over a quarter of the machinery is outdated and needs to be renovated or replaced (AmCham 2004b: 70).

The textile industry is no longer dominated by the public sector, as it was from the time of the nationalisations of 1960–61 until the late 1990s. By 2003, 10 per cent of spinning, 40 per cent of weaving, 60 per cent of knitting, and 70 per cent of garment enterprises were privately owned, operating alongside 10 cotton ginning and trading companies and 29 spinning and weaving companies affiliated with the state's Cotton and Textiles Holding Company (AmCham 2004b: 24). The share of the private sector has recently increased, as several textile firms have been privatised since the Nazif government took office in July 2004, and higher value and higher quality products are now dominated by private enterprise. In response to the crisis in spinning and weaving, production of ready-made garments has expanded and become the most dynamic element in the textile industry, replicating developments in the late nineteenth and early twentieth centuries, when competition from imported European cloth led to a decline in Egyptian spinning and weaving but a sharp rise in clothing production (Chalcraft 2004: 55–8). According to AmCham, in 2004 public-sector firms employed about 120,000 workers, while private sector firms employed about 143,500 workers (AmCham 2004b: 25, 28; CAPMAS 2001). While available statistics are contradictory, it appears that the industry accounted for about a quarter of all manufacturing employment.[5]

A combination of labour costs and inadequate capital investment rendered the Egyptian textile industry globally uncompetitive in the 1980s and 1990s, resulting in lower production and reduced investment. By 2004 textiles and apparel declined to 27 per cent of the value of industrial production, taking second place behind processed foods (AmCham 2004b: 20). Textiles and apparel comprise about 25 per cent of all non-oil exports and 15 per cent of all commodity exports (AmCham 2004b: 21). In order to flourish, the industry must export successfully and compete with China, the rising star in the global textile and clothing industry. This translates directly into downward pressure on wages. The average wages of Egyptian textile workers are already among the lowest in the world: in 2004 they were about half those of its major North African and Middle Eastern competitors in Morocco, Tunisia and Turkey but higher than those of Asian competitors such as Bangladesh, China, India, Indonesia and Pakistan (AmCham 2004b: 33–4).

Wages and conditions in the neoliberal era

In 2008 the minimum wage for industrial workers was E£108.50 a month. According to AmCham (2004b: 33), the average basic monthly wage for textile and clothing workers in the first half of the first decade of the twenty-first century was E£250. In the public sector, incentives, allowances and bonuses raised the gross monthly wage to E£400–450. Today workers in public-sector enterprises work daily shifts of eight hours, six days a week, and receive time-and-a-quarter for overtime.[6] Precise information about wages and working conditions in private-sector enterprises is difficult to come by. According to the manager of a well-run private-sector textile enterprise, in 2005 a weaver earned about E£1,000 a month (including basic pay of about E£500–600 plus incentives); a spinner earned about E£800 a month (including basic pay of about E£400 plus incentives). Private-sector textile workers work 12-hour shifts.[7]

While legally required to provide the same social benefits and health insurance as public-sector firms (services with a current cash value of some E£400 a month), only a small minority of private firms do so; others evade the law by bribing inspectors and producing for the local market, which requires lower standards of documentation than for the export market. All firms must pay a severance package equal to two months' wages for every year worked if they dismiss a worker. Firms which successfully avoid paying social insurance benefits are able to fire workers freely because there is no official record of their employment with the government – a strong additional incentive for illegal behaviour.[8] It is widely reported that before being hired in a private-sector enterprise workers must sign undated letters of resignation so that they can be dismissed without receiving severance pay if they 'make trouble'.

The 2003 Unified Labour Law legalised indefinitely renewable fixed-term contracts (Posusney 2003). This means that many workers remain in limbo for years, living in fear of exercising their rights and without job security. Although 1991 legislation forbade mass lay-offs after privatisation of a firm, managers of public-sector firms under consideration for privatisation often attempt to make them more attractive by reducing the workforce before sale. A survey of sixteen firms privatised since 1995 indicated that only two of them – Al Ahram Beverages, privatised in 1997, and the San Stefano Hotel, privatised in 1998 – have increased the number of their employees, despite receiving significant new capital investment.[9] The Assiut Cement Company, where the workforce was reduced from 3,774 to 865 after it was privatised in 1999, is an extreme case of the more common trend (Knight 2007). In the mid-1990s anxieties about unemployment and other possible consequences of privatisation prompted a renewal of strikes and collective action (Pratt 1998). These were not idle fears: the official rate of unemployment climbed sharply from about 8 per cent during 1990s (see Chapter 2 for estimates of the current level).

Workers under the Nazif government

The holders of economic portfolios in the government installed in July 2004 were western-educated Ph.D.s and businessmen in the entourage of Gamal Mubarak, son of the president.[10] They promoted a second wave of privatisation and enacted other measures to encourage foreign direct investment, such as reducing to zero the tariffs on textile machinery and spare parts (AmCham 2006). In addition in December 2004 Egypt concluded a trade agreement with Israel and the USA which created Qualifying Industrial Zones (QIZs – see Chapter 8).[11] Fears about loss of jobs and the unwillingness of new private investors to pay fringe benefits or contributions to retirement funds were the main motivation for new collective actions that began soon after Nazif took office. The strike wave, which began in 2004 and continues in 2009, is the largest social movement Egypt has witnessed in over half a century. Over 1.2 million workers and their families have engaged in some form of action in the context of political ferment that began with a taboo-breaking demonstration in December 2004 organised by Kefaya, the Egyptian Movement for Change (see Chapter 5). According to the 2004 annual report of the Land Center for Human Rights (LCHR), from 1998 to 2004 there were over 1,000 workers' collective actions, of which more than a quarter occurred in 2004 alone, a 200 per cent increase over 2003 (Beinin 2008). There were 74 actions in the first half of 2004 – but 191 following the installation of the Nazif government in July. Some 25 per cent were in the private sector, a larger proportion than ever before.

The workers of the Egyptian–Spanish Asbestos Company (Ora Misr), established in 1983 in Tenth of Ramadan City, organised one of the more dramatic of such actions. Ora Misr manufactured building materials using asbestos for over twenty years after the substance was banned in the USA and Europe; between 1997 and 2004, 18 workers (including two managers) died, 46 contracted lung cancer, and many of the 120 remaining on the job suffered from asbestosis (Rady 2005b). CTUWS filed a complaint with the International Labour Organisation (ILO) in June 2004. Under pressure from the LCHR, the ILO, other Egyptian NGOs and French trade unions, in September 2004 the government belatedly fined Ora Misr, and ordered its closure and payment of compensation to its workers. Its owner, Ahmad Luqma, fired all the remaining workers without paying them. In November 2004 workers set up an encampment outside the gates of the closed factory and remained there for over nine months; in July 2005 some of them occupied the headquarters of ETUF and successfully pressured the organisation to support their demands (Rady 2005b).

A further protracted struggle at the ESCO Spinning Company in Qalyub, north of Cairo, put the renewed drive to privatise the public sector into the spotlight. ESCO workers were highly conscious of their role in confronting the reorientation of Egypt's economy as part of the 1991 ERSAP agreement (Beinin 2005b). By 2005 their numbers in the six ESCO mills had been reduced to 3,500 through a combination of attrition, a hiring freeze (after the 1986 strike referred to above) and five waves of early retirement packages. In October 2004, after they saw a press report announcing the prospective sale of the Qalyub spinning mill to a private investor, some 400 ESCO workers struck briefly to protest against privatisation. If the privatisation took place, they wanted their jobs to be guaranteed; if that was not possible, they sought adequate early retirement packages. On 13 February a second strike began. Mohamed Gabr 'Abd Allah, spokesperson for the workers, explained that in 1999 the company was valued at E£60 million. In 2003 the government invested E£7 million in capital improvements, including computerised spindles. It then concluded a three-year lease agreement for E£2.5 million a year with an Egyptian businessman, Hashim al-Daghri. Before his lease expired al-Daghri bought the mill at a bargain-basement price of E£4 million.

ESCO workers believed that they and the broader public were the real owners of the enterprise, not the state managers. Gamal Sha'ban, a skilled worker with twenty-three years seniority asked, 'With what right was the sale [of this mill] conducted?' (Beinin 2005b). Many ESCO workers had twenty to thirty years' service and believed that this entitled them to retain their jobs rather than be replaced by new workers likely to receive lower wages and benefits. The second dispute lasted four months and, after an open-ended hunger strike, ended on 12 May. The result was a partial workers' victory: seasonal contracts guaranteeing enforcement of the 2003 Unified Labour Law, E£10,000 per worker in lieu of an early retirement package, and back pay for three months (Rady 2005a). The strike set the tone for many that followed in the public sector. While ESCO workers were unable to stop privatisation, they achieved economic gains well beyond anything striking workers had achieved in the 1980s or 1990s – and workers elsewhere received the message that strikes might achieve real gains. LCHR reported 202 workers' collective actions in 2005, 222 in 2006, and a staggering 614 in 2007.[12] During 2007 strikes spread from their centre of gravity in the textile and clothing industry to encompass building materials workers, transport workers including those on the Cairo Metro, food-processing workers, bakers, sanitation workers, oil workers in Suez, and many others. Private-sector workers comprised a more prominent component of than ever before. In the summer of 2007 the movement broadened to encompass white-collar employees and civil servants.

The single largest collective action of the entire movement to date was the December 2007 strike of some 55,000 real-estate tax collectors employed by local authorities. After months of public demonstrations, they struck briefly and won their demand for wage parity with counterparts employed directly by the Ministry of Finance.[13] The government formally conceded to the workers' demands (Carr 2008a). Of far more lasting importance, a year after the strike nearly half the tax collectors, led by their elected strike committee, formed the first trade union independent of the regime since 1957.

Mahalla al-Kubra

The largest and most politically significant industrial strike since a dispute in the same workplace in 1947 took place in December 2006 at the Misr Spinning and Weaving Company in Mahalla al-Kubra, where nearly a quarter of all public-sector textile and clothing workers are employed. On 3 March 2006 Prime Minister Nazif decreed an increase in the annual bonus given to all public-sector workers, from E£100 to two months' salary. The last time annual bonuses were raised was in 1984 – from E£75 to E£100. 'We read the decree, and started spreading awareness about it in the factory', said Mohamed al-'Attar, one the leaders of the strike, 'Ironically, even the pro-government labour union officials were also publicising the news as one of their achievements.'[14] He continued: 'December [when annual bonuses are paid] came, and everyone was anxious.

We discovered we'd been ripped off. They only offered us the same old E£100. Actually, E£89 to be more precise, since there are deductions [for taxes].'

Over the following two days, groups of workers refused to accept their salaries and a fighting spirit was in the air. On 7 December, thousands of morning-shift workers assembled in Tal'at Harb Square, facing the entrance to the mill. Production ground to a halt when around 3,000 female garment workers left their stations. They marched to the spinning and weaving sections, where their male colleagues had not yet stopped their machines, and stormed in, chanting 'Where are the men? Here are the women!' Ashamed, the men joined the strike. Around 10,000 workers gathered in the square, shouting 'Two months! Two months!' Black-clad Central Security police were quickly deployed around the factory and throughout the city, but did not act to quell the protest. 'They were shocked by our numbers', said al-'Attar, 'They were hoping we'd fizzle out by the night or the following day.' Management offered a bonus of twenty-one days' pay but, as al-'Attar laughingly recalled, 'The women [workers] almost tore apart every representative from the management who came to negotiate.' As night fell, said Sayyid Habib, another of the strike leaders, the men found it difficult to convince the women to go home: 'They wanted to stay and sleep over. It took us hours to convince them to go home to their families, and return the following day.' Grinning broadly, al-'Attar added: 'The women were more militant than the men. They were subject to security intimidation and threats, but they held out.'

On the fourth day of the occupation panicking government officials offered a 45-day bonus and gave assurances that the company would not be privatised. The government also promised that, if the company earned more than E£60 million in profits during the year, 10 per cent of profits would be distributed to the workers. The strike was suspended, with the government-controlled trade-union federation humiliated by the success of unauthorised action. This victory reverberated throughout the textile sector, and in subsequent months thousands of workers in at least ten mills in Alexandria and the Delta participated in protests ranging from strikes and slowdowns to threats of collective action if they did not get what the Mahalla strikers won. In almost all cases the government conceded.

Gender issues

The proportion of females in the formal industrial labour force is low in Egypt by both regional and global standards. In the neoliberal era, however, it has increased markedly: from 10.9 per cent in 1981 (917,000) to 22 per cent in 2002 (4.3 million). This is largely due to economic necessity: two-thirds of all Egyptian families cannot survive on a single income, while the number of women-headed households reached 25 per cent by 1995. At the same time the unemployment rate for females rose from 19 per cent in 1981 to 24 per cent in 2002 (Shukrallah 2006: 31–6).

Women workers are concentrated in textiles and clothing manufacturing and in the lowest paid positions: 35 per cent of all textile and clothing workers are female, far outstripping the 8.5 per cent in medical products and 6.5 per cent in food processing (Shukrallah 2005: 36). Women cluster in the ready-to-wear apparel sector, which pays lower wages.[15] Women have played an especially prominent role in several strikes in both public- and private-sector enterprises. At Misr Spinning and Weaving in Mahalla al-Kubra they were the key force that set off the work stoppage and sustained its militancy. Women also played a leading role at the Mansura-España Garment Factory during the events of April to June 2007. Mansura-España opened in Talkha as a private firm in 1985 but did not do well, despite receiving orders from the giant American corporation Wal-Mart from at least 2003 to 2006.[16] It became indebted to the United Bank, which consequently acquired the company. The firm did not pay bonuses or profit dividends to its workers from 1999 to 2006, and during 2006–07 the workforce was reduced from 1,200 to 284 (Stack 2007). In response to rumours that the company would be liquidated and its land sold, the remaining workers, three-quarters of them female, undertook a sit-in strike. The women, who earned basic pay of E£135–150 a month, were desperate to keep the enterprise open and save their jobs: several went on a hunger strike, and five threatened to commit suicide. The strike concluded with an unequivocal victory, United Bank pledging either to invest new capital or to sell the firm to a buyer who would agree to maintain production without dismissing any workers or cutting their wages.[17] However, the Bank and the government failed to uphold any of their commitments. In March 2009 production had ceased; the workers were on strike again and still struggling to keep the factory open.[18]

The small, largely female workforce was too weak and too far from the centre of media attention on the workers' movement to sustain their victory. Nonetheless, the strike was an extraordinary demonstration of the power of women workers. Their supposed 'docility' and 'traditional' background did not inhibit active participation in the strike: a front-page photo in *Al-Misry Al-Yawm* featured the women in hijab (headscarf) and niqab (full concealing veil) standing shoulder to shoulder in solidarity with their male colleagues.[19]

From bread to politics?

Soon after the December 2006 Mahalla strike its leaders launched a campaign to impeach local union officials who had opposed the strike and who, according to activists, enjoyed close ties with the security services. Eventually, over 13,000 workers signed a petition addressed to the General Union of Textile Workers demanding impeachment of the local union committee and new elections. ETUF bosses opposed the impeachment demand because it suggested that trade unions should actually represent workers rather than constitute an arm of the state. Consequently workers began mailing their resignations to the General Union of Textile Workers.

The idea of a trade union independent of the state apparatus began circulating among trade unionists in the 1990s and is supported by many progressives in the labour movement. Government repression, questions about the legality of independent trade unions, and internal divisions about tactics and strategy among the forces involved, produced great uncertainty about whether insurgent forces had the organisational capacity to launch a parallel trade union. One element of the government's strategy to discredit the workers' movement is to accuse either the Muslim Brothers or the communists of inciting actions. There is no evidence that the Brothers played an organised role in any labour protest during 2004–08; there are apparently internal differences within the organisation between affluent businessmen who dominate the leadership and rank-and-file members from the lower middle classes and working poor (see Chapter 6). This may explain why Muslim Brother MP 'Abd al-'Aziz al-Husayni announced his backing for the February 2007 walkout of the Misr Spinning and Weaving workers in Kafr al-Dawwar and why parliamentary colleague Sabr Abu al-Futuh from Alexandria (where the organisation is particularly strong) also issued several statements supporting the spring 2007 Arab Polvara strike.[20] Abu al-Futuh coordinated the Brothers' campaign to run candidates in the Autumn 2006 trade-union elections. He had declared that if the elections were rigged the Brothers would establish a trade union independent of the regime, similar to the independent student unions established in cooperation with the Trotskyist Revolutionary Socialist group at several universities. Yet, after the first rounds of voting were over and their undemocratic character was apparent, the Brothers' Deputy General Guide Mohamed Habib sounded more reserved: 'Establishing an independent labour union requires a long period of consistent organising', he said. 'Workers are different from students because they have family responsibilities and will not lightly risk their livelihoods.'[21]

All the parties of the left were present in the strike movement, though its leaders insist that the great majority of them do not belong to any political organisation and regard political parties with suspicion. Although strikers received news of their colleagues' triumphs with enthusiasm, there was no evidence of logistical coordination among workplaces. However, there were some signs that following successful strikes militant textile workers were seeking a mechanism of national cooperation. A month after the victory of the strike in Kafr al-Dawwar a statement signed by 'Workers for Change in Kafr al-Dawwar' was distributed in the factory, calling for 'expanding coordination between workers in companies that went on strike with us, to create the necessary solidarity links and exchange experiences'. Nonetheless, despite several attempts, textile workers have been unable to organise regular meetings of activists seeking to establish an independent trade union.

Misr Spinning and Weaving II

Despite mounting repression directed against opposition forces of all stripes, in September 2007 the Misr Spinning and Weaving workers struck for the second time in a year – and won. As they did in December 2006, the workers occupied the mill and rebuffed the mediation efforts of the NDP. The second strike was even more militant than the first, belying the claims of the Egyptian government and much of the media that the strike wave had run its course. The dispute was impelled by unfulfilled promises made at the conclusion of the December 2006 strike. Workers then accepted annual bonuses equal to forty-five days' pay rather than the two months' pay they had been promised the previous March. Published figures indicate that Misr Spinning and Weaving made between E£170 million and E£217 million in profit in the fiscal year that ended in July 2007. Workers claimed that they were due bonuses equal to 150 days' pay, though they received the equivalent of only 20 days' pay. After a six-day strike they won an additional 70 days' bonus pay, payable immediately. A meeting of the company's administrative general assembly after the strike was to increase this to a total of at least 130 days' pay. Much-hated CEO Mahmud al-Gibali was eventually dismissed. The biggest victory of the Misr workers was in the political arena, however: after first refusing to meet the workers, regime representatives including ETUF chief Husayn Mugawir were forced to come to Mahalla to negotiate with the elected strike committee, bypassing the official trade-union committee. Thus, while the Misr workers did not formally win their demand to impeach the trade-union committee, they rendered it irrelevant.

In contrast to most other collective actions since 2004, in September 2007 some of the Mahalla strike leaders explicitly framed their struggle as a political contest with national implications. Sayyid Habib announced 'We are challenging the regime.'[22] Chants and banners raised during the strike opposed the economic policies of the Nazif government. Worker Karim al-Buhayri, who writes the widely read Arabic blog *Egyworkers*, uploaded video clips featuring workers chanting 'We will not be ruled by the World Bank! We will not be ruled by colonialism!'[23] Mohamed al-'Attar, one of eight leaders arrested for two days during the strike, told journalists:

> We want a change in the structure and hierarchy of the union system in this country… The way unions in this country are organised is completely wrong, from top to bottom. It is organised to make it look like our representatives have been elected, when really they are appointed by the government.

Later that day he told a pre-*iftar* (Ramadan breakfast) workers' rally:

> I want the whole government to resign.... I want the Mubarak regime to come to an end. Politics and workers' rights are inseparable. Work is politics by itself. What we are witnessing here right now, this is as democratic as it gets. (Stack and Mazen 2007)

Such statements indicate that the workers' movement had begun to adopt a culture of protest and to contribute to the formation of a consciousness of citizenship and rights far more effectively than anything that party politics or NGO work has achieved.

A broad popular mobilisation against inflation in early 2008 that was closely linked to the strike movement presented opportunities for the oppositional middle-class intelligentsia to link up with the workers' movement. The second Mahalla strike served as a rallying point for all the opposition forces. But, for the most part, these opportunities were missed.

On 17 February some 10,000 workers and their families in Mahalla al-Kubra, many of them waving loaves of bread, demonstrated against soaring prices, especially of basic foodstuffs, which rose 33 per cent (for meat) and 146 per cent (for chicken) from 2005 to 2008.[24] Mahalla workers were in the forefront of a movement demanding a national minimum wage of E£1,200 a month to cope with this inflation, embarrassing the ETUF leadership into advocating an increase of E£800 a month. The rising cost of living also impelled doctors and university professors to threaten strikes, lending broader legitimacy to the workers' movement and further discrediting the Mubarak regime. The Mahalla workers called for a strike on 6 April to support their national minimum wage demand. Massive repression and intimidation by the regime successfully split the workers' leadership and aborted the strike. Since then, some of the same leaders who had been most open to framing their demands in explicitly political terms have been less willing to do so.[25]

The Mahalla workers and the independent tax collectors' union are the most organized and politically aware elements of the working class. But they are not yet able to play a larger role in the movement for democracy in Egypt, despite the vacuum in the leadership of that movement since 2007.[26] The future of the workers' movement is undecided. However, the combination of repression, apathy and political demobilisation which sustained autocracy in Egypt for over half a century has been challenged, making it unlikely that the Mubarak regime will be able to continue indefinitely with business as usual.

5

The democracy movement: cycles of protest

Rabab El-Mahdi

New currents

For decades political activists in Egypt have been denied all opportunity to express their views in public. The print media have been closely controlled, while rallies and lobbies have been banned under the Emergency Law and those who dare to organise demonstrations or marches have been victims of assault, arrest, imprisonment or worse. But since 2000 voices of dissent have been heard and a series of movements has successfully created a bridgehead for self-expression. In 2004 democracy activists began to contest the apparently comfortable hegemony of the Mubarak regime. The Egyptian Movement for Change, known by its slogan Kifaya ('Enough!'), and its sister groups, together known as Harakat al-Tag'eer (Movements for Change), attracted much attention in Egypt and abroad. They broke many taboos, bringing to the scene people new to politics and challenging a view widespread outside the Middle East that the Arab world is intrinsically resistant to democratisation. But the movement appeared to rise and fall abruptly, causing frustration and bewilderment among some participants and many observers. What accounts for these rapid changes, and what are the implications for the wider society?

Egypt's democracy movement is often seen as mysterious – as having emerged without warning and as disappearing without trace.

This is especially marked in the European media: in Britain the *Guardian*, for example, comments on 'the grassroots Kifaya movement, which came from nowhere' (Black 2007), while in Germany *Der Spiegel* suggests that 'the 'Movement for Change', or Kifaya, has disappeared into oblivion' (Follath et al. 2006). In fact the movement can be understood as one loop in a chain of continuous currents of protest known in the literature on social movements as 'cycles of protest',[1] which have maintained different but complementary activities. These have been sufficiently important to mark a distinct period in contemporary Egyptian politics – one that is far from over.[2]

The movement emerges

Since the 1952 *coup d'état*, successive Egyptian constitutions have allowed presidents to ensure 're-election' through referendums in which the sole candidate is nominated by parliament. This procedure is at the centre of an authoritarian state system controlled by a single political organisation tied to the presidency. The ruling party/organization has had various names – al-Hay'aat al-Tahrir (Liberation Agency), al-Ittihad al-Qawmi (the National Union), al-Ittihad al-Ishtiraqi (the Socialist Union) and most recently al-Hizb al-Watani al-Dimuqrati (the National Democratic Party, NDP). The last emerged in 1976 as one of a series of organisations within a notionally multiparty system. In fact it inherited all the powers of the earlier monoliths (see Chapter 1). Each of Egypt's three long-term presidents has come from the inner circles of the party, which continues to control what Brownlee (2007: 3) calls 'one of the oldest authoritarian regimes in the developing world'.

In eight parliamentary elections held between 1976 and 2005 the NDP maintained a comfortable majority in the Majlis al-Shaab (People's Assembly, the lower house of parliament), repeatedly presenting its candidate for presidential office on the basis of an assured success. In 2004, shortly before a referendum which would mark Mubarak's fifth six-year term in office, there was a loud demand for change. The Popular Campaign for Change ('Freedom Now') and Kifaya were the first of many groups 'calling on President Mubarak not to seek a fifth term and ... rejecting the prospect that Gamal Mubarak, the president's younger son, would "inherit" power' (Shehata, 2004:

4). They included Women for Democracy ('The Street is Ours'), Youth for Change, Journalists for Change, Artists for Change, and Workers for Change. Despite differences, underlying principles were shared by these groups, of which the most important were rejection of a further mandate for the president, opposition to dynastic succession within the Mubarak family, and a commitment to electoral democracy.

On 12 December 2004 Kifaya held its first – silent – demonstration. This came less than three months after the idea for a new campaigning group and the slogan 'Kifaya!' had first been discussed at a dinner by seven veteran activists, including Marxists, Nasserites, Islamists and Liberals.[3] The movement went on to organise a host of public activities – demonstrations, campus rallies, meetings and marches. Its strategy of political disobedience meant that activists risked arrest and abuse, and police tactics sometimes isolated demonstrations so completely that they went unseen and unheard (riot police formed vast concentric circles around protestors so that only the most determined activists reached assembly points). Nonetheless, a year after its establishment, Kifaya had accumulated some 1,800 signatures on a founding statement – a significant index of support in a society in which public expression of dissent has long implied close attention by the security services (Kifaya 2004). The statement set out principles for democratic reform:

> We, the undersigned, are citizens of Egypt; are part of its rich social texture; and are active in its public life in different arenas: intellectual, civic, political, cultural, and unionist. We come from different walks of life and together represent Egypt's rich political diversity. We believe there are two grave dangers which beset our nation today. They are two sides of the same coin, each nourishing the other, and neither curable alone. (Kifaya 2004)

The twin dangers, said the organisation, were 'the odious assault on Arab native soil [Palestine and Iraq]', and a 'repressive despotism' pervading all aspects of the Egyptian political system, and which required reform:

- termination of the current monopoly of power at all levels, starting with the seat of the President of the Republic;
- effecting the rule of law as the supreme source of legitimacy;

- elimination of the current unfounded [economic] monopoly and squandering of the wealth of the nation;
- regaining Egypt's legitimate and significant, if now lost, place among the family of nations (Kifaya 2004).

Hundreds of young people, most new to politics, were soon drawn into activities that received headline coverage in local and international media. Beinin (2007: 11) comments that although Kifaya's national organisational capacity was limited, 'the slogan ['Enough!'] caught on in Egypt and abroad. For... two years the movement inspired myriad offshoots.' Kifaya had made its mark, leading Mubarak to attack the movement by name, alleging that it was a foreign initiative and that those who attended its protests received payments to participate. 'What Kifaya does is paid for,' he said, 'I could have organised paid demonstrations to shout "not enough".'[14] (Critics responded that the comments revealed much about Mubarak's own approach to political mobilisation – see Chapter 1.)

Young activists of the movement challenged the regime in novel ways. Moving from street protests in city centres to informal mobilisation in working-class areas of Cairo such as Shubra and Sayyida Zeinab they undertook 'guerrilla' actions in which timing and assembly points were organised through text messaging and the Internet. Azimi (2005) describes the approach of Youth for Change:

> Groups of two to four activists visit public squares or parks, erect mini-exhibitions with flyers, and engage people on the street in impromptu discussion (their internal motto is *kilamateen wi bas* or 'two words is enough'). In seeking to link daily concerns with failures of the political process, activists broach issues that touch all sectors of life – from transport costs to healthcare access to unemployment.

In an important development, young people made extensive use of blogs and activist websites dedicated to arranging demonstrations, disseminating information about arrests and charges, and debating strategy and tactics. Levinson (2005) describes the emergence of 'an online community that acts as a virtual megaphone for Egypt's burgeoning opposition', noting the speed with which e-networks became integral to the opposition movement. Blogs initiated during the early phases of the movement have since become part of the political landscape in Egypt. By 2007 there were said to be 6,000 active bloggers, among whom a minority addressed political issues but with an impact disproportionate to their numbers (Saleh 2007).

Facilitated by e-communications which allowed activists to outwit the police, several demonstrations marched through popular areas unchallenged – the first such public protests for over fifty years. In June 2005 Hamla Sha'biya min Agl al-Tag'eer (the Popular Campaign for Change) brought together some 500 activists in Shubra near central Cairo. Here they walked through crowded shopping streets and markets raising slogans most residents had never heard in public: 'Kifaya, Kifaya', 'Down with Mubarak' and (with reference to the visit of US Secretary of State Condoleezza Rice) 'Give Husni a visa – take him with you Condoleezza.'[5] Onlookers blinked in disbelief: some joined the march; most watched while young men apparently supporting the government challenged demonstrators, who replied with taunts of 'Ya 'eshreen geenah, bet'ulu eh?' – 'Hey twenty pounds, what are you saying?' (implying that the 'counter-demonstrators' had been paid to attend). Such events did not draw mass support, as activists had hoped; they nonetheless maintained a momentum the regime found difficult to contest, so that some such marches went ahead without the usual police presence. One young activist commented that participating was 'like meeting a date and finding that the partner is a no-show'.[6]

Sociologist Asef Bayat, who has long studied street life in Cairo, comments that such an event 'not only brings together the invitees but also involves strangers who might espouse similar, real or imagined, grievances... It is this epidemic potential, and not simply the disruption or uncertainty caused by riots, that threatens the authorities who exert a pervasive power over public spaces.'[7] The protestors were in effect vectors of the contaminating demand for change: their mere presence in public was enough to cause alarm among those accustomed to controlling the streets.

Origins of the movement

The horizontal structure of Kifaya allowed for much local enterprise. At the leadership level decisions were taken by consensus in a steering committee composed of several tendencies: the Karama Party (Nasserist); the Ghad Party (Liberals); the Centre Party and the Labour Party (Islamists); and the Revolutionary Socialist Organisation. With the exception of the Ghad, all were illegal (unlicensed by the state).[8] Even the Ghad was a breakaway from the historic (and deeply compromised) Wafd Party (its leader Ayman Nour faced charges levelled by the state that he had forged his organisation's founding documents; he had been jailed in January 2005). Kifaya drew in members of traditional opposition parties including the Wafd and the formally leftist al-Tagammu', although there was no coordination with the latters' leaders, seen within the movement as complacent and lacking in popular support. Kifaya was in effect a consortium of new activists who breathed life into Egyptian politics.

What made this development so significant? In the early 1990s Mubarak had attempted to close down formal politics, using both the Emergency Law and a series of restrictive acts introduced under the pretext of contesting Islamist activity (Kienle 2001; Schwedler and Clark 2006). For the rest of the decade there was little open public opposition to the regime and most academic analyses concluded that active interest in change had subsided. Brownlee, for example, observed that 'Mubarak has subdued Egypt's Islamists, leftists, and human rights community to the point where there is little domestic impetus for reform' (2002: 11). The new activism marked a definite break with the preceding period. The focus of mobilisation, the range of groups involved and the stress on political participation were also novel developments. For decades activity in the workplaces and on the streets had been driven by economic or regional concerns; now political reform, even though not delinked from the former, was the central issue around which a wide range of groups and individuals came together, challenging the legacy of inaction of legal opposition parties.[9] Kifaya seemed to confirm that any challenge to the regime, if not the political system at large, would come from outside the matrix of established political organisations.

The rise of the movement can best be understood through what literature on social movements calls 'spill-over effects'. Meyer and Whittier (1994: 277) comment that movements are seldom distinct and self-contained; 'rather, they grow from and give birth to other movements, work in coalition with other movements, and influence each other indirectly through their effects on the larger cultural and political environment'. Interviews with leading activists in the Egyptian movement, as well as participant observation of its emergence and growth, suggest that Kifaya was in fact a 'third cycle' of activism that followed closely upon earlier movements – the pro-intifada mobilisations of 2000–2001 and the anti-war movement of 2003. W. is a leading activist in the both Kifaya and the Anti-Globalization Egyptian Movement (AGEG), his anonymity preserved for security reasons. He comments:

> The protest movements [in 2004] came as a third stage of protests, following the pro-intifada demos which were the first street demonstrations we saw in more than a decade. Then there were the demos against the war in Iraq. A momentum was definitely beginning to build up and both movements, pro-intifada and anti-war, though they started out with solidarity slogans, ended with slogans against Mubarak, the police, and the system as a whole. Following the antiwar demos of 20 and 21 March 2003 the police were especially brutal... this was the first time that different political groups began to openly think about doing away with Mubarak, a matter that was not clearly or explicitly mentioned before.[10]

The second Palestinian intifada, which began in September 2000, marked the start of a new era of Egyptian street politics. As Pratt (2007: 170) observes, 'The second *intifada* triggered perhaps the largest and most radical spontaneous demonstrations in the Arab world since the first Gulf war'. In Egypt thousands of students took to the streets, breaking an iron rule of the regime that their voices should never be heard outside the walls of their campuses, if at all. They included young people from the elite and highly secluded American University in Cairo (AUC), attended by many sons and daughters of senior officials of the regime. High-school students also participated in large numbers, with numerous eyewitness accounts of demonstrations in schoolyards and in streets across the country. Sadiki (2000: 83) comments that the intifada soon took on 'a spiritual importance in the eyes of the millions of Arabs, epitomizing hope that people-power resistance might one day enable disaffected Arabs to achieve their objectives of justice, equality, and emancipation'. Egyptians were no exception: the solidarity movement provided an opportunity for broad sectors of the Egyptian masses, especially students, to practise expression of disenchantment towards the regime through demonstrations, on-campus activities and boycott campaigns directed against Israel and its American ally.[11]

The intifada brought collective political action back to the streets; it also pushed new actors into establishing innovative collaborative forums. Moved by the mood for action, in 2000 a group of twenty NGOs and independent activists of diverse backgrounds established the Popular Committee to Support the Intifada (PCSI). For the first time in modern Egyptian history, the committee had members of rival political factions – Muslim Brotherhood members, Nasserists and Socialists – as well as activists from professional syndicates and NGOs. Over the next two years it collected the equivalent of $400,000 in donations, food and medical supplies for convoys to Palestine (a huge sum in the context of popular politics in Egypt), and gathered more than 100,000 signatures on a petition calling on the government to cut diplomatic relations with Israel.[12] It managed to overcome ideological differences and historical grievances and to translate popular sympathy for the Palestinians into mass campaigns. According to Aida Seif El-Dawla, a founding member of the PCSI and of the Popular Campaign for Change,

> For some time the experience of the Popular Committee was so inspiring... it was a movement that we wanted to recapture later on when pushing for an umbrella pro-democracy movement that integrated different political factions.[13]

Following the model of PCSI a number of campaigning groups came into existence, including AGEG, 20 March Movement for Change, and the Defence Committee for Labour Rights. Regardless of the specific mandate of each, their appearance was of paramount importance, providing forums for engagement of activists outside the discredited party platforms. They also provided space for continued contact and collaboration among activists, offering opportunities for self-education in negotiation, tactics, and means of overcoming ideological divisions in the interest of achieving shared aims – especially important when street activities came to a halt due to intensified repression. These forums were also structures through which activists began to gain a sense of changing boundaries for mass participation and street mobilisation: it is no coincidence that leading figures such as Kemal Khalil, Aida Seif El-Dawla and Hamdeen Sabahi were also initiators and leaders of the democracy movement which was soon to emerge.

After a low point in 2002, when campaigns and street-based activities in support of the intifada lessened in intensity, a new mobilisation took place in response to the invasion of Iraq. On 20 March 2003 activists called a demonstration in central Cairo, expecting a few hundred to attend but drawing over 40,000 people to Tahrir Square. The regime hesitated, apparently fearful that its usual violent response might generalise a demonstration which had already declared (echoing words of a song by the poet Salah Jahin) *'al-shari' lina'* – 'the street is ours'. Protestors occupied the square for over 24 hours in what soon became known as a Tahrir intifada before security forces could disperse them. One account suggested that 'Cairo had witnessed two days of protests like nothing seen since the 1970s':

> Normally a snarl of honking traffic that pedestrians cross at the peril of death, the square belonged to the demonstrators on that day. For about 12 hours, they wandered almost bemused across its suddenly car-less expanse. 'This is the first time we've made it out of the cage', said one jubilant activist. Riot police were present in vast numbers, but only on the edges of the square. They had surrendered the center, which was filled with some 3,000 people listening to speeches and chanting slogans … anti-regime slogans filled the air. (Schemm 2003)

Over the following days university campuses around the country as well as potential assembly spaces – mosques, squares and student residences – were surrounded by armoured security cars and riot police. After many arrests and two further abortive demonstration attempts in which police attacked participants with extreme violence, the initial mobilisation subsided. The change of mood and growth of confidence, however were there to stay, together with a renewal of traditions of 'the street' which had once been a hallmark of Egyptian politics.

Cycles of protest

Early demonstrations for political liberalisation, starting in December 2004, involved many participants from the pro-Palestinian intifada and anti-war demonstrations, together with newcomers brought by these activists.[14] Not only did the nascent movement capitalise on leadership and mobilisation structures of earlier campaigns but it also energised shared communities of protest. A cycle of contestation had emerged in which each phase of activity was related to earlier actions and to the responses of the state. The democracy movement should therefore be understood in the context of a series of mutually reinforcing initiatives within which shared networks and overlapping leaderships grew in confidence, learning strategy and tactics and developing a space in which they could overcome their ideological differences. This is not to suggest that the movements were merely a creation of leading political actors and the 'spill-over' effects of their initiatives. Each was prompted by specific circumstances and by the continuing structural crises of the Egyptian economy and state system, which had long since alienated the mass of the population. The trajectory of each movement, however, was shaped by a process of repeated reinforcement – and this was soon to have further implications.

Structures and agency

How is it possible to explain the rise of the democracy movement in the period preceding the 2005 referendum – why not before or after? The reductionist answer that some versions of social movement theory would offer, that its participants saw an opportunity in the upcoming elections, does not suffice, since this was not the first plebiscite during Mubarak's reign. Nor was the rise of the movement preceded by a relaxation in the authoritarian environment. The emergence of the movement, including its actors (who came from outside mainstream political parties), can best be understood in light of cycles of contention that preceded it and energised it through shared personnel and leadership, through communities of protest, through collectively learned tactics, and through creation of a space for overcoming ideological divisions. The rise of the movement is also an indication of changing structural factors, including the waning of Mubarak's legitimacy due to his pro-American/Israeli role in the region and deteriorating living conditions associated with intensification of neoliberal reform. It is these changing structural conditions, along with the engagement of new political actors, that continued to provide an environment for public dissent, even after the waning of the pro-democracy movement.

Kifaya was a litmus test for the regime's resilience, identifying the limits of reform and measuring its willingness to use repression. After an initial tolerance of limited pro-democracy protests, in March 2005 the regime started to show its more violent face, reacting aggressively to demonstrations called in a number of cities with the involvement of the Muslim Brotherhood. Participants called for political reform, in line with Kifaya, and were met with tear gas and brutal beatings from police. At least one, Brotherhood member Tarek Ghannam, was killed after an attack by riot police in Daqahlia; hundreds were arrested (Howeidy 2005b). Kifaya activists were also affected by the state's renewed turn to violence. On 25 May 2005, during a protest against the suggested amendment of Article 76 of the constitution, female protestors were subject to organised sexual harassment by security forces.[15] Numerous reports by international media carried vivid descriptions of the violence. The correspondent of the the *Washington Post* described a rampage by police and officials of the NDP:

> Officials of President Hosni Mubarak's National Democratic Party, or NDP, led hundreds of young men who attacked anti-government demonstrators. Journalists and witnesses at the scene of several incidents, including this correspondent, saw riot police create corridors for stick-wielding men to freely charge the demonstrators. Women were particular targets, with at least five pulled from the mass of mostly male demonstrators on the steps of the Journalists' Syndicate in central Cairo and subjected to slaps, punches, kicks and groping. The blouses of at least two were ripped. (Williams 2005)[16]

In the following months prominent public figures, including Islamist thinker Mohamed Al 'Awa, judge Tariq El-Bishry, ex-minister Yehia El-Gamal and ex-prime minister Aziz Sedki, established the National Front for Change. This called on the Mubarak regime to step down, criticising both its economic and its political policies. Meanwhile a Front for Saving Egypt was established in London by Egyptian businessmen and professionals in Europe. While the mass-mobilisation capacity of these new organisations remained limited, they gave further impetus to the democracy movement, challenging regime supporters among the middle class and among loyalist intellectuals. At the same time they gave legitimacy to campaigns for political liberalisation as forms of activism which were both worthy and productive. During the summer of 2005 a further initiative, the

National Coalition for Change, was undertaken jointly by socialists, the (Islamist) Labour Party and the Muslim Brotherhood. It proposed an unprecedented move towards formal and systematic collaboration between people of radically different political persuasions – on an organisational rather than an individual level. There was soon intense debate about the wisdom and even the ethics of such a strategy, especially on the left.

Neither development – defection of regime supporters and new liaisons between opposing political forces – has since produced more than statements, press conferences and rallies. Kifaya had originally hoped to organise a demonstration of 100,000 participants and stage acts of mass civil disobedience.[17] But, as Hamzawy put it:

> Despite their relative success in reinventing the street as an arena for political action, nascent protest movements remained largely ineffective in terms of constituency building due to their limited appeal outside urban centers. Kifaya and its heirs clearly could not mobilize significant segments of the Egyptian middle class. (Hamzawy 2005: 4)

The impact on wider political mobilisations has been significant, however. Although Kifaya's initiatives never drew more than several hundred, they nevertheless prompted questions about how groups can represent and organise among millions alienated from the regime. Agreement on political liberalisation and regime-change by ideological adversaries has brought an authority of consensus to the disparate forces of the opposition. People with radically different aspirations – ranging from the secular socialist state to the Islamist theocracy – have agreed on the need to end Mubarak's rule. This important development is a specific outcome of democracy activism, introducing to the Egyptian political scene the much-needed 'united front' – what recent literature on social movements calls 'cooperative differentiation'. Abdel-Rahman comments:

> One of the major tactics which rising global movements, characterized by coalition-building adopt, and which is clearly present in the Egyptian case, is that they develop a means of ensuring 'cooperative differentiation', whereby they 'maintain a public face of solidarity towards the movement's targets while differentiating themselves in communications with their constituencies' (Bandy & Smith 2005: 10). This allows for diverse political groups with different ideological leanings, class interests, and long-term projects to work together. (Abdel-Rahman 2009: 40)

Under conditions of extreme authoritarianism and with a history of fragmented opposition, as in Egypt, this promises much for political liberalisation and for wider change. While it remains a focus of debate on the left and the right, this approach had been manifested in practice in support of a host of socio-economic struggles. In the case of the strike movement, for which no political group in Egypt can claim an initiating role, activists from the left who have seldom worked together now collaborate effectively in solidarity campaigns.[18]

Kifaya's aftermath

After the presidential elections of 2005, Kifaya and its sister movements began to fade and other actors moved to centre stage. In 2006 Egypt's judges mobilised for independence of the judiciary – an unprecedented development in which dissent came from within the core structures of the state itself. The judges made a potent case against the regime, alleging corruption and malpractice within the electoral system and demanding freedom from political influence. Under the constitution, judges are required to certify election results. Nadi al-Quda (the Judges' Club), a semi-official association for the judiciary, refused to endorse the parliamentary elections of 2005 after more than a hundred of its members reported irregularities at the polls (see Chapter 1). Two of the country's leading judges, Mahmud Makki and Hisham al-Bastawisi, members of the country's senior court, had been vocal in condemning electoral fraud. In February 2006, they were stripped of judicial immunity and charged with 'defaming the state' in disciplinary hearings. The case attracted enormous international attention: Human Rights Watch (2006a) commented that 'The government is punishing judges just for doing their job. It should be investigating the widespread evidence of voter intimidation, not shooting the messengers who reported the fraud.'

Members of the Club organised a sit-in at their premises in Alexandria and later in Cairo. When they appeared for trial at the High Court demonstrators gathered in support, identifying the accused as symbols of their own aspiration for change: crowds chanted 'Judges, judges, save us from the tyrants' (BBC 2006). Many protestors, the majority of them having been active earlier under Kifaya, were attacked with great brutality: over 250 were arrested. In addition, the

Muslim Brotherhood joined mass protests: in May 2006 their demonstrations brought downtown Cairo to a halt. Independent observers reported furious assaults on activists as well as on journalists and film crews. Human Rights Watch commented (2006b): 'The government is apparently determined to stamp out peaceful dissent – literally. It seems that President Mubarak sees growing popular support for the reformist judges as a real challenge to his authoritarian ways.'

Enter the workers

As the judges' campaign subsided (one of the accused having been found not guilty, the other reprimanded) a new wave of activism developed, this time among workers and professionals. After decades of silence, industrial workers began a series of strikes which were to continue for several years, encompassing almost every area of the economy, public and private (see Chapter 4). The events involved historic centres of working-class militancy such as the textile mills of Mehalla al-Kubra, extending to include – for the first time – entire sectors of white-collar state employees, namely the tax collectors. Most demanded increased wages and/or improved contracts, bonuses and job security. Several disputes brought rank-and-file workers into sharp conflict with the official trade-union machinery – in effect into conflict with the state. The liberal daily newspaper *Al-Misry Al-Yawm* reported that during 2006 there were 222 sit-in strikes, stoppages, hunger strikes and demonstrations; between January and April 2007 the paper noted a new labour action almost every day (Beinin and Hamalawy 2007) During the first year of socio-economic protest over 100,000 workers were involved, 'the largest social movement in Egypt in over half a century' (Beinin 2007: 20).[19]

Although the democracy movement cannot claim direct links to workers' activities through organisational coalitions, overlapping constituencies or shared personnel, the rise of the workers' movement cannot be dissociated from its influence. As one of the most important accounts by participants in the workers' movement asserts, the activities of Kifaya and associated groups have been of profound importance:

> It is impossible to disregard the effects on the workers of recent
> political transformations that Egypt has witnessed: from the outburst of

the [Palestinian] intifada in September 2000 to the latest constitutional amendments, and in between the invasion of Iraq in 2003, amendment of Article 76 of the constitution and the presidential and parliamentary elections. As part of society, the working class is affected by what happens around it. The political mobilization that earned the right to demonstrations and confronted the security has definitely shaken the status quo [which has been] stable for decades. (El-Bassiouni and Saeed 2007: 6)

Workers' struggles which followed the apparent demise of the pro-democracy movement have an organic connection with the latter. Brownlee (2007: 149) sees a close relationship: 'Kifaya's demonstrations varied in size from dozens to hundreds but seemed to embolden other groups to articulate their criticisms and manifest the depth of their popular support.' The democracy movement acted as a test balloon, exposing the limits of the regime's 'liberalisation' measures and political reforms and its capacity to resist popular demands for change. Kifaya introduced new mechanisms to the political process that transgressed the movement itself. Though not fully successful it deepened collaboration among oppositional actors and strengthened politics from below, introducing tactics that have been taken up by others to great effect.

Conclusion

Generalisation of economic, political and social protest has produced an unprecedented rise in the numbers – and diversity – of Egyptians expressing disenchantment with the regime's policies. They include activists in all manner of industries and state services: parents staging sit-ins in protest at school conditions in remote villages; slum-dwellers displaced by urban clearance schemes; mothers on hunger strike against police torture of their children; scores of villages and towns marching to demand access to clean water. As McAdam et al. (2001: 4) observe, a 'dynamics of contention', in which 'different forms of contention – social movements, revolutions, strike waves, nationalism, democratization, and more – result from similar mechanisms and processes', can be observed in action.

The fact that unorganised public expression of grievances began in 2006 suggests a correlation between rising expressions of dissent and the democracy movement. In this respect, even though Kifaya and its sister groups did not constitute a mass movement in terms of size and constituency, they did produce what Kuran (1989: 42) calls 'the spark for prairie fires'. A regime may be privately hated while it seems to enjoy public support – an expression of reluctance by most citizens to publicise their opposition. It may seem unshakeable until even minor shocks reveal its vulnerability, encouraging a 'bandwagon' process in which a panoply of social conflicts, until then largely hidden, become apparent (Kuran 1989: 42).

Correlation between diverse movements is not necessarily an outcome of direct processes of political learning or the work of joint constituencies, but can also be an outcome of 'example-setting'. In the case of Egypt, media coverage of the democracy movement, together with widespread discussion of its initiatives in workplaces and communities, extended the menu of alternatives and possibilities. Kifaya, together with the movements which preceded it, facilitated expression of disenchantment and brought confidence that collective action could highlight specific causes and predicaments. The rising protest movement provided a new channel for politics. By offering alternative means for organising dissent, the movement has contributed to the Egyptian political sphere and to the potential for affecting regime change.

The Egyptian state is likely to face further cycles of popular opposition, especially as it approaches presidential elections in 2011 under the shadow of the international financial crisis. Challenges are certain to arise within the domain of political rights and democratisation, although – and perhaps specifically because – the democracy movement of 2005 *did not* achieve a decisive advance. Not compelled to make a full retreat, the activists and sympathisers of Kifaya and its sister movements remain ready to re-engage and to pass on their experiences, while Egypt's working-class movement continues to assert itself: what makes a further cycle of protest more challenging for the regime is indeed that its prelude would be the strongest labour movement witnessed in five decades. This promises an unprecedented field for expansion of the pro-democracy movement, both qualitatively and quantitatively. At the same time it challenges a renewed pro-democracy movement to build organic links with participants in the continuing wave of socio-economic protests.

6

Islamism(s) old and new

Sameh Naguib

The growth of political Islam is undoubtedly one of the defining features of Egyptian society and politics over the past three decades. During the early 1970s the leading role in opposition to the regime was played by leftist and secular nationalist forces; religiously inspired groups were politically marginal and relatively insignificant. By the first decade of the twenty-first century a dramatic shift had taken place, with political Islam having become the dominant oppositional force. Among students and in professional syndicates and poor urban neighborhoods, Islamist organisations had become practically hegemonic. Whereas the secular opposition was able at best to mobilise 2,000 people in the pro-democracy demonstrations which began in December 2004, in the following months the Muslim Brotherhood mobilised tens of thousands of its supporters throughout the country (see Chapter 5). The parliamentary elections of November 2005 demonstrated a similar tendency. The Brotherhood won eighty-eight seats, nearly 20 per cent of parliament, despite the fact that it presented only 150 candidates and was severely restricted by the regime's security forces, especially in the third round of voting. In contrast the secular opposition, including Nasserists, Leftists and Liberals, won fourteen seats – just over 3 per cent of the total.

The growing influence of the Brotherhood over the past three decades is part of a broader growth of Islamism both in Egypt and in the region. In Egypt this has also included the emergence and spread of more militant armed Islamic groups, notably the Gama'at Islamiyya (Islamic Groups)[1] and the Jihad organisation; the proliferation of non-political Islamic groups such as Tabligh and Dawa; and the growing influence of Islamic writers, thinkers and preachers not directly affiliated to any particular group. How do we explain this shift in Egyptian society and politics? In examining these changes this chapter will focus on the experience of the Brotherhood, by far the largest, most organised and politically successful of the Islamist trends. How was it possible for Islamism in general and for the Brotherhood in particular to transform itself from a fringe phenomenon in the early 1970s to the largest opposition force in the country by the first decade of the twenty-first century? How does this relate to the changing socio-economic and political context within which this movement expanded? How has the changing context, on the one hand, and the expansion of the movement, on the other, affected the discourse, ideology and programmes of the movement? This chapter will attempt to provide preliminary answers by critically exploring some of the most influential interpretations of Islamism as they apply to the Brotherhood, and to provide an alternative account of its growth and transformation.

Interpretations

The rapid growth of Islamism in Egypt and the region in the past three decades has led to a plethora of theories and interpretations. On the left, academics such as Samir Amin (2001) and Gilbert Achcar (1981, 2004) have seen the movement as representing a segment of the ruling class connected to Arabian Gulf capital and import–export businesses, viewing its main thrust as reactionary and anti-democratic. For Achcar, 'fundamentalists', including the Brotherhood, have constituted for the Egyptian regime an ideal 'fifth column' inside the wider society – and a particularly effective counter to the Left. On this view the Egyptian regime's attitude towards the 'fundamentalist' movement resembled that of any ruling class faced with a deep social crisis, which it tackled by moving towards the far Right and fascism.

The Islamic movements, according to this reading, are the result of a bourgeois mobilisation of segments of the petty bourgeoisie, in alliance with the state, with the aim of weakening the Left.[2]

Such readings of the growth of Islamism, especially when applied to the Brotherhood, tend to generalise about the movement from its situation at a particular historical conjuncture. They ignore the shifts and transformations in the social composition of the movement, as well as the social, economic and cultural contexts within which it developed. Both the pre-Nasserist history of the movement[3] and the developments of the 1980s and 1990s show the extent to which an organisation such as the Brotherhood has represented different social groups at different moments in its development. Its history is full of shifts, contradictions, and both systemic and anti-systemic features. Hence, 'freezing' the movement at a particular historical conjuncture leads to an ahistorical and mechanical reading that does little justice to the critical and historical schools to which such writers belong. As I will attempt to demonstrate below, the Brotherhood has been in a constant state of flux as internal contradictions and changes in the social composition of the movement have forced changes in its strategy, tactics, discourse and programmes.

More recently a number of studies exploring Islamism in terms of social movement theory (SMT) have emerged.[4] The most relevant to the case of Egypt is Carry Wickham's (2002) study *Mobilizing Islam*. Wickham sees the Islamic movement as consistent with Tarrow's definition of social movements: 'collective challenges, based on common purposes and social solidarities, in sustained interaction with elites, opponents and authorities' (Tarrow 1998: 4). Accordingly, she examines how since the late 1970s the Brotherhood was able to mobilise its recruits under authoritarian rule, arguing that the erosion of state capacity for control expanded the 'structure of political opportunity' for the organisation on the social and political periphery of the ruling order.

By using SMT as a tool in analysing the growth of Islamism in Egypt, Wickham has shown that this form of contentious collective action is not simply an outcome of accumulated grievances but also hinges on the success of movement efforts at mobilisation. She has also addressed assumptions of Islamic exceptionalism and essentialism that have so often marred social studies of Islamism. There are several weaknesses in this approach that need to be addressed, however. First, as Bayat has argued, 'the concerns, focus and even the direction of movements may change over time as a result of both internal and especially, external factors' (2005: 897). A related problem arises from the difference between the relatively open political context in the West and the authoritarian context in countries such as Egypt. As Bayat (2005: 892) puts it, 'democratic conditions and movements often breed internal difference and dissent, since the availability of both means and opportunities allows for an open, clear and dissenting exchange of ideas.' Since this is not the case in the Egyptian context, the apparent unity and homogeneity of the Brotherhood and the generality of its political slogans conceal a plethora of different and conflicting interests.

Post-modernist critique

Another set of interpretations of the rise of Islamism in the past three decades focuses exclusively on the cultural dimension of the movement, in particular as it relates to the perceived crisis or failure of Western modernity. In this sense, the growth of Islamism answers to a need for difference, cultural independence, and an alternative ideological framework and challenge to that represented by the dominant Western secular modernity and its claim to universality. Thus Burgat and Dowell (1993), for example, describe the Islamist movements in the Middle East as the third phase of the anti-colonial struggle after the political and the economic, focusing on the cultural dimension of independence. A similar approach was put forward by the prominent Egyptian historian Tariq al-Bishry (1983), for whom the previous waves of anti-colonialism neglected the cultural and civilisational aspect of independence. This created a serious weakness, which partially explains, for example, the failure of the Nasserist experiment.

On a more sophisticated level, some post-structuralist writers have seen the growth of Islamism as parallel to the growing post-modernist critique of Western modernity since the Enlightenment.[5] Thus Sayyid (2003) analyses the phenomenon as part of the 'decentring of the west' and the delinking process between the 'West' and 'modernity'. It is therefore seen as a further challenge to the claimed universality of

Western historical processes. The strength of such cultural interpretations lies in their critique of linear universalist and modernisation accounts which see the rise of Islamism as a result of the failure to achieve secular modernity.

There are several weaknesses, however, which make such interpretations of limited use in understanding the complexities and contradictions of the rise of Islamism. For example, one of the most widely used slogans of the movement in Egypt – 'Islam is the solution' – can mean completely different things to different currents and actors within the same movement. Differentiation is not only between a weakening hegemonic Western modernity and an emerging counter-hegemonic Islam; it is also a battle of ideas *within the movement itself* and within the social contexts in which the movement emerges and grows. For while an industrial worker joining the Brotherhood might conceptualise an Islamic 'solution' in terms of social justice and equality, a businessman could view the same 'solution' in terms of law, order and social and economic conservatism. A related problem is the eagerness of many post-structuralist accounts to overcome reductionist assumptions of economistic accounts of Islamism by focusing exclusively on culture. Hence questions of class, the contradictions of capitalist development and the shifting context of both local and global economies are discarded and we are left with a cultural 'essentialism of difference' that oversimplifies both the internal contradictions of Islamic movements and the dynamics of change within them.

Another approach to the growth of Islamism has been to use the concept of populism. This concept has often been used to describe Islamism either in terms of a substitution for earlier forms of secular nationalist populism or in terms of a specifically petty-bourgeois populism reacting to the contradictions and failures of the post-colonial secular state. Thus Abrahamian (1992) sees a movement of sections of the middle class that succeeds in mobilising the poor with radical slogans directed against imperialism, foreign capitalism and the political establishment. While these movements promise national independence and better living conditions, they stop short of threatening the principles of private property. Zubaida (1993) also explains the success of these modern populist movements in terms of the failure of previous secular versions. According to Zubaida, the masses rallying to Islamism could as well support nationalist or socialist movements, if the latter had not failed in opposing imperialism, and if 'their leaderships and ideologies' had not been 'subordinated to and utilized by the ruling cliques and ... consequently tainted' (Zubaida 1993: xviii).

There are two particular problems with such approaches. First, they do not explain why it was Islam in particular that acted as a unifying ideology for such movements. It is not sufficient to cite the failure of the previous secular alternatives since this becomes a tautological argument – Islamism succeeded because non-Islamism failed. Second, some such approaches, by limiting these movements to the interests of a particular class, usually some version of the petty bourgeoisie, end up ignoring the contradictions and varied tendencies and conflicts within such movements.

Diversification of the Islamists

As a result of some of these misinterpretations a number of groups labelled 'Islamist' have mistakenly been seen as part of the same movement; in fact such groups have shared little more than the label. Even within one organisation such as the Brotherhood there is little continuity. It is important to note that the Brotherhood of the 1970s was fundamentally different in social composition, political discourse, and strategy and tactics from the pre-Nasser Brotherhood of the 1940s. By the end of that decade it had become the largest political mass movement in the country – despite its ardent anti-communism and its real (though short-lived) alliances with politicians linked to the monarchy and with conservative nationalists of the Wafd party. It played a major role in the anti-colonial struggle, challenging the historical hegemony of the Wafd, and putting forward social and economic programmes that included substantial land reform, nationalisation of the Suez Canal, and state-led economic development (Mitchell 1969, Lia 1998). By the 1970s, however, the remnants of the Brotherhood had lost all links with their former social base and the grassroots membership of the Nasser era. From a mass movement of nearly 500,000 members in the 1940s it had become a group of a few hundred, strongly linked to Saudi Arabia, and among which many had become wealthy businessmen as a result of Sadat's *infitah*, joining a tactical alliance with Sadat against perceived threats from the left.

When Brotherhood leaders who had been jailed under Nasser were released in the 1970s they began a regroupment around the monthly magazine *Al Dawa*, under the leadership of Omar Tilmisani and with the tacit approval of the regime. The politics of *Al Dawa* and the strategy and tactics of the new Brotherhood were associated with the social composition of the new grouping. The content of the magazine was openly anti-Semitic, anti-communist and anti-secular; it also carried advertisements which made clear its links to the new Islamic financiers of the Sadat era (Kepel 1985). *Al Dawa* was clearly in support of Sadat's liberalisation policies; its only reservations related to the moral implications and the problems of a perceived Western 'cultural invasion'. All the social and economic policies of the Nasserist era, including land reform and nationalisation, were severely criticised as 'communist' measures that had led to the 1967 defeat (Utvik 2006). The social composition of the Brotherhood at this period, and its openly reactionary discourse on women and on Egypt's Coptic minority, lend credibility to the characterisations of Amin and Achcar. In fact, according to a study by Saiid, by the 1980s the private sector of the economy was controlled by eighteen families, of which eight were connected to the Brotherhood: some 40 per cent of all private economic ventures, she suggests, were connected to Brotherhood interests (Saiid 1989: 23).[6]

Independently of the Dawa group another significant regrouping and growth of Islamism was under way – one that was to have a decisive influence on the nature of the Brotherhood. With the tacit support of the Sadat regime small groups of Islamist students began to challenge leftist influence within the student movement. Islamist student associations organised a rapid and successful recruitment campaign and soon won leadership of the most important campus unions. In 1976 they secured leading positions at Cairo and Minya universities and by 1979 had won the majority of seats on the board of the general student union at a national level (Wickham 2002: 116). Within a few years they had displaced the left as the main expression of student anger and opposition: their phenomenal growth meant that the student associations went far beyond acting as a control mechanism in the service of the regime.[7]

Student Islamists initially avoided overt political issues, concentrating their efforts on student services and moral and religious issues. As

Essam Al-Erian, one of the founders of the Islamic student associations in the early 1970s describes the situation: 'We concentrated on providing services to students. The Leftist students concentrated on national political issues so we did not have any competition in the area of services' (Al-Erian 2004: 2), Yet, as their influence and numbers grew, and as the political context changed, a rapid process of politicisation took place. This became apparent when in 1979 Sadat agreed a peace treaty with Israel. The Islamic associations led opposition to the treaty and to Sadat's perceived abandonment of the Palestinian cause. Al Erian records that student associations organised mass meetings to oppose both Sadat's peace policy with Israel and his speeches on the separation of religion from politics (Al-Erian 2004). At the same time Sadat began to recognise the threat posed by growth of the Islamists, particularly as the leftist challenge was rapidly receding.

Two distinct tendencies eventually emerged from the student Islamic associations of the early 1970s. The first and by far the largest and most influential was that led by Essam Al-Erian and Abdel Meneim Abu Al-Futuh, which merged with the Dawa group and became part of the new Muslim Brotherhood. They severed their ties with the second tendency, composed of radical *jihadi* groups influenced by the ideas of Sayed Qutb. The result of the merger between the first tendency and the Brotherhood was to begin a process of change in the latter's political, ideological and social outlook. For the first time since the 1940s the Brotherhood had regained its roots among educated youth and began to rebuild a mass movement. Meanwhile the *jihadis* renounced the gradual reformist strategies propagated by the Brotherhood. Basing themselves on the prison writings of Sayed Qutb (who had been executed under the Nasser regime in 1966), they advocated a strategy of direct action and confrontation with the state. For the Brotherhood, reformism meant using legal political space to contest elections in professional syndicates and local and national assemblies. The *jihadis* vehemently opposed such a strategy, accusing the Brotherhood of providing legitimacy to the state and leading the movement towards accommodation and defeat. According to Abud El-Zumur, one of the leaders of Islamic Jihad: 'The government carefully responds to some of the limited demands of Islamists inside parliament to fulfil its containment conspiracy to the point of convincing Muslims that there is a possibility of applying Islamic law through the assembly' (Ahmed 1995: 287).

For the *jihadis* only direct action and violent confrontation with the regime could achieve the imposition of sharia law and the establishment of an Islamic state. The practical implication of this logic was that the Gama'at Islamiyya began building organisationally in areas in which the state apparatus had least control and where its own radical rhetoric would have the most resonance, notably impoverished towns of the South such as Assiut and Minya, and in the shanty towns in Cairo and Giza. Three main tactics were employed in these areas. The first was to use private mosques to propagate the group's message and recruit new members: by the mid-1980s the Gama'at controlled around 150 mosques in the Assiut district of Dairut alone. The second tactic was to deploy direct action groups for the local imposition of sharia law. Under the label of 'forbidding vice' these groups attacked stores selling videos or alcohol, segregated the sexes in public spaces, enforced Islamic dress codes on women, and attacked Coptic churches and shops they considered both an obstacle to imposing sharia and an issue on which the regime was vulnerable (Mubarak 1995). The third tactic was provision of social services. With the entrenchment of the neoliberal economic model and the retreat of the state from the realm of social services, the Gama'at Islamiyya began organising social services through the mosques, finding a wide clientele for food distribution schemes, school supplies and health clinics.

At the same time the *jihadi* groups became more confrontational. They stimulated sectarian conflicts at the local level; targeted religious figures associated with the regime; and eventually assassinated the president himself in 1981. During this period the regime became less tolerant of the Islamists; following the assassination Mubarak cracked down on the groups but soon adopted a more permissive policy, and during the 1980s the *jihadi* movement was able to expand into the slums and poor districts of Greater Cairo such as Ain Shams, Al-Zawiya al-Hamra and Imbaba. It was only in the early 1990s that the state shifted from a policy of what might be called permissive repression to one of violent elimination. In May 1992 over 2,000 soldiers were deployed in the Assiut district of Dairut, imposing a curfew and a state of emergency. In December of the same year 16,000 troops were sent into the Giza slum of Imbaba to eliminate the local base of the movement. The national crackdown that ensued included mass arrests, with some 47,000 detained between 1992 and 1997, and widespread use of torture, hostage-taking, assassinations and executions (Mubarak 1995). It is only in this context of unprecedented state repression that we can understand the cycle of violence that engulfed Egypt during the 1990s and was to result in over 1,400 deaths and several thousand injured (Mubarak 1995).

In response to the crackdown the movement attempted an all-out assault against the state, targeting policemen, security forces, government officials, tourists and banks. There was also an unprecedented escalation of attacks against the Coptic community, with over fifty attacks during 1992 and 1993 alone (Mubarak 1995). The cycle of violence culminated in the massacre of fifty-eight tourists by members of the Gama'at Islamiyya in November 1997. The attack was to prove the last major assault by the movement: the state repression that followed effectively eliminated the radical organisations, whose leading cadres were assassinated, executed or imprisoned. By the end of the decade the mosques which formed their mobilising base had been shut down or placed under strict government control. Their social base had meanwhile been fragmented by the repression and by their own alienating and extreme practices of 'forbidding vice' in poor neighborhoods.

Transformations of the Brotherhood

With the demise of the *jihadi* movement, which had never been as influential as the Brotherhood, the latter became the only significant trend of political Islamism. Not only is the Brotherhood the most important organisation relative to other Islamist groups; it has become the most important opposition movement and the only mass-based political movement in Egypt. Following the merger of the student groups with the Brotherhood in the 1970s, the organisation was able to become the leading force in the student movement, and soon achieved domination of the professional syndicates, winning the support of hundreds of thousands of their members. In 1984 it began participating in elections of the doctors' syndicate, gaining 7 of 25 seats on the governing board. By the 1990 elections it had gained 20 seats on the board and 71 per cent of all votes cast (Wickham 2002:

184). Similar successes were achieved in the engineering, dentistry, pharmacology and agriculturalist syndicates. Eventually even syndicates dominated for decades by secular political forces, such as the lawyers' and journalists' syndicates, had significant Brotherhood representation. This was a logical extension of the latter's success in the universities: automatic enrolment of university graduates in the professional syndicates meant that Brotherhood members found in them a new political space to exercise the organisational and activist skills acquired as students.

These developments were closely associated with general socioeconomic change. The syndicates had been transformed by a massive expansion of university education – once elite organisations, they had become mass institutions with hundreds of thousands of members. The rate of expansion of university education, and therefore of the number of university graduates and members of professional syndicates, far outpaced the growth of employment opportunities for those graduates. Most graduates expected government jobs through the guaranteed employment scheme introduced by Nasser in the 1960s (see Chapter 2). From the mid-1970s, however, the waiting period between graduation and employment grew longer: by 1979 it was three years and by 1985 it had become ten years (see Handoussa 1991). At the same time the private sector, despite growing in relative strength due to economic liberalisation, was not able to absorb the growing numbers of graduates. The hegemony of the Brotherhood within the syndicates meant that a significant segment of educated urban society had been won over as activists or supporters. But it also meant that the discourse and social messages of the Dawa group of the 1970s were no longer appropriate for the new and growing audience of impoverished graduates gravitating towards the Brotherhood. The leadership in the professional syndicates began advocating a message of equity, social justice, moral renewal, criticism of official corruption and neglect of the common welfare (Wickham 2002: 157–62).

A reading of the Brotherhood's development exclusively in terms of mobilising the 'lumpen intelligentsia' or its appeal to a disgruntled petty bourgeoisie fails to register the extent to which the organisation transformed itself into a populist political force, attempting to move beyond the confines of its student and graduate cadre. Parallel to its work in the universities and professional syndicates, the Brotherhood expanded its mass base in poor neighbourhoods. Private mosques, Islamic charities and NGOs were utilised as 'mobilising structures' to activate a growing network of cadres and to win new influence. As the regime accelerated its neoliberal policies and the state retreated from providing basic services, the Islamists were able to fill the vacuum, creating a mass base of supporters that included not only disaffected students and graduates but also workers and sections of the urban poor. More importantly, they won support by providing services previously accessed through the state and by beginning to position themselves as a political, cultural and economic alternative to a regime that combined commitment to neoliberalism and alliance with the West with a fierce authoritarianism.

The Brotherhood's success was soon reflected politically in parliamentary elections, prompting a severe crackdown by the regime. This included removing elected boards in the syndicates and subjecting leading members of the organisation to military tribunals and imprisonment. Despite successive waves of repression, however, the Brotherhood continued to grow in influence. In the 2000 parliamentary elections, despite widespread fraud and police intervention, eighteen of its candidates were elected as independent members of parliament; in the 2005 elections, again despite severe security restrictions, its representation increased to eighty-eight seats.[8]

Contradictions for success

For thirty years the Brotherhood has undertaken a series of shifts in discourse, strategy and tactics. In what follows I focus on three key areas: economic policy, nationalism and democracy.

Economic policy

As we have seen, the Brotherhood was generally supportive of the liberalisation policies of the Sadat regime and continued through the 1980s to call for more extensive market reform – a position it maintained until the early 1990s. As the state accelerated its neoliberal reform programme by means of a structural adjustment programme agreed in 1991 with the IMF and World Bank, contradictions began to emerge in the Brotherhood's economic discourse. On one hand, central planning and state ownership were criticised. The public sector was characterised as plagued by low productivity, bureaucratic central planning, waste, corruption, and unstable priorities and policies (Al-Ghazali 1990). When the Brotherhood turned its attention to industrial workers, however, a different discourse was employed, so that in the trade-union elections in 1991, notes Beinin (2005: 133), its candidates 'supported the right to strike, criticized the neoliberal economic programme for Egypt, opposed government interference in the trade union elections, and opposed the wholesale liquidation of the public sector'.

Further contradictions became apparent as the regime embarked on an accelerated neoliberal programmme including privatisation of state-owned industries and utilities, abolition of subsidies on basic goods, and further liberalisation of foreign trade. In the electoral programme produced in stages by the Brotherhood from 2004 and published before the 2007 Shura elections (for the upper house of the Egyptian parliament), the privatisation programme was criticised strongly for dissolving the public sector and reducing the capacity of the state to play its role in modernising the economy. The programme also criticised the state for abandoning its role in providing basic services and welfare, listing rights the state should guarantee for all citizens, including a minimum sufficient standard of living for poor families, the right to free medical care and basic education, social security rights, and entitlement to pensions. It observed:

> The role of the state should continue to be pivotal for any future vision of total and sustainable development. If the state does not play its role, this will have a negative effect on development and economic well-being and might lead to social chaos and economic collapse... Private production is not suitable for some commodities that require the intervention of the state and the public sector. (Muslim Brotherhood 2007: 39)

The central role of the state in the economy, earlier seen as a source of evil, has became a major element in the Brotherhood's programme. This does not mean that the organisation has abandoned its free-market convictions: in the document quoted above it is not privatisation in itself that is the target of critique; rather, it is the means of privatisation and the scale on which it has been pursued which receives critical attention. According to the Brotherhood, the regime has failed to reach a balanced view of the role of the state during transition to a market economy.

These contradictions arise not only from the practice of pragmatism but more importantly as a response to the organisation's varied and changing social base, within which some elements have conflicting interests. As the state moves forward with economic reform, and as wider sections of the poor and the middle class are adversely affected, the Brotherhood has attempted to incorporate a populist critique of neoliberalism in its erstwhile pro-market discourse. An organisation which includes hundreds of thousands of the 'lumpen intelligentsia' is also home to millionaires such as Khairat El-Shater (deputy general guide) and Hassan Malek. In formulating its economic vision the organisation is subject to forces which pull both directly and indirectly in different directions.

Nation and nationalism

During the 1970s opposition to the regime's alliance with the United States and to its peace agreements with Israel was led by the secular left; by the 1990s, however, the Brotherhood had become the champion of the Palestinian cause and the focal point in Egypt of resistance to American aggression in the region. Its role in supporting the first Palestinian intifada and its strong links with Hamas, which was rapidly replacing Fatah as the leadership of the Palestinian national liberation movement, added to the popular appeal of the Brotherhood as a staunch defender of the Palestinian cause. Similarly, the Brotherhood vehemently opposed the entry of American forces into the Gulf region and the subsequent war on Iraq in 1991. It attacked the Gulf regimes for allowing foreign armies on Arab and Muslim lands, warning that these forces 'would come to stay and that this was a new return of military occupation in the region' (Al-Erian 2003). This angered the Saudi regime, and its minister of the interior made statements attacking the Brotherhood. One result was that the organisation lost both funding and political links with the pro-American Gulf regimes.

But the Brotherhood is neither consistently anti-imperialist nor prepared to take the confrontation with the regime over its regional role to a logical conclusion. In the absence of secular forces prepared to resist the new American hegemony in the region, the organisation has nonetheless filled a vacuum, leading mass opposition towards both the American war on Iraq and Israeli brutality against the Palestinian people. As it tries to balance pressure from its mass base for more radical anti-imperialist positions with that from its influential bourgeois membership for more 'realistic' foreign policy positions, the vacillating nature of the Brotherhood leadership is reflected repeatedly in contradictory statements. On the Palestinian question, leading Brotherhood figures have assured the 'international community' that on coming to power they would abide by treaties signed by the current regime, including the Camp David accords. Other statements have meanwhile assured members and supporters that they would never recognise treaties with 'Zionist gangs usurping the land of Palestine' (Akef 2007). Similarly, during the 2006 Israeli war against Lebanon, the general guide announced that the Brotherhood was prepared to send 10,000 trained fighters to the aid of Hizbullah – a declaration that other leaders later described as being of a 'metaphorical' nature.[9]

Democracy

These contradictions are no less pronounced in the Brotherhood's discourse on democracy. In the 1970s the organisation was vague about what the term meant and how it related to the Islamic concept of *shura* – and was clearly reactionary on the rights of women and the Christian minority, and on the extent of individual and institutional freedom of expression in any future Islamic state. As it became more involved in parliamentary and electoral politics, however, and as the state continued to use emergency laws, military trials and brute force to limit the space available to the Islamists, democracy took on new meanings.

Parliamentary democracy, full political freedoms and an end to all exceptional laws became central planks of the Brotherhood's message and campaigns. *Shura* and liberal democracy became synonymous in its literature and the Brotherhood became the largest and most effective force in the shortlived pro-democracy movement of 2004–06 (see Chapter 5), with tens of thousands of its supporters engaged in demonstrations and thousands arrested. Equal citizenship rights for men and women and for Christians and Muslims has also become a familiar slogan on the lips of Brotherhood leaders. When the latest version of their draft political programme was put forward for discussion, however, it contained blatant contradictions on democracy and rights. On the one hand, the programme states categorically that all citizens have equal rights, regardless of religion or gender; on the other hand, it insists that neither women nor Christians can run for the position of president of the Republic of Egypt – the contradictions involved becoming a subject of heated debate within the Brotherhood.[10] As with other major contradictions, this was not simply an issue of opportunism or confusion but an outcome of continuing struggle by the leadership to cohere disparate social groups that make up the organisation's cadre and support base.

Conclusion

Contradictions in the strategy, tactics and discourse of the Brotherhood, and repeated changes in the social composition of the organisation and its base, must be set against continuity in the organisation's orientation on Islam as a unifying factor. The central slogans of the Brotherhood – 'Islam is the solution', 'the Islamic state', and 'the enforcement of sharia' – have remained constant throughout a history which goes back to the late 1920s. Significantly, in 2007 the subtitle of its programme for parliamentary elections was: 'Yes, Islam is the solution.' Since the 1970s this idea has been central to all the Brotherhood's electoral interventions and has been a major target of criticism on the part of its opponents – usually on the grounds of ambiguity and vagueness, or on the basis that implicit within it is a critique of other programmes as being un-Islamic, implying political opportunism on the part of the Brotherhood. Such readings of this theme seem to miss the point: it is the nature of the Brotherhood's contradictory and varied social composition that makes such general ideological signifiers essential.

The very abstractness of these signifiers, in particular their ahistorical nature, provides them with a plasticity that makes it possible to unite disparate social groups. 'Islam' becomes the solution to all problems: to injustice and exploitation suffered by workers and the poor; to the national humiliation and personal alienation experienced by the educated middle class; to the lawlessness and disorder feared by the rich; and even to the degradation and harassment suffered by young women in work or on the street. The 'Islamic state' is seen as a kind of social-democratic welfare structure that will provide justice and dignity to the workers; at the same time it is an ultra-conservative and reactionary utopia in which women, workers, minorities and others are taught to listen and obey. Such flexibility allows the Brotherhood to carry both counter-hegemonic and hegemonic impulses and tendencies. This is both a strength and a weakness of mass populist movements. It acts as a strength, but only as long as the leadership is able to balance different impulses and to avoid concrete actions that would explode a fragile unity. In conditions of extreme repression and in political and social crises, however, this is not enough to prevent vacillation and confusion that can soon threaten disintegration of the movement.

7

Torture:

a state policy

Aida Seif El-Dawla

Amnesty International (2002) warns that 'In Egypt everyone taken into detention is at risk of torture.' Since 1981 Egyptians have lived under an official State of Emergency which provides police and security agencies with powers to prohibit demonstrations, censor newspapers, monitor personal communications, detain people at will, hold prisoners indefinitely without charge, and send defendants before special military courts to which there is no appeal. In 2008, at least 18,000 prisoners were being held as 'administrative detainees' – some had been incarcerated for more than a decade, despite repeated rulings in the civil courts that they should be released (Amnesty International 2008b). In this state of 'lawlessness' security forces act with impunity, with the result that ill-treatment and torture of ordinary Egyptians has become a systematic, daily practice (Human Rights Watch 2008b).

As this chapter is being written, farmers are being attacked by police backing landlords who demand eviction of tenant cultivators; the Central Security riot force is using tear gas and rubber bullets against protestors who oppose the sale of state-subsidised wheat to business corporations; and people arrested in demonstrations for political change are being detained without charge, despite orders for their release. In 2007 Egypt was elected to the United Nations

Human Rights Council, following a specific pledge to lift the State of Emergency and implement 'full realization of human rights and fundamental freedoms for all... the promotion of democracy, rule of law and good governance' (Human Rights Watch 2008c). In May 2008 Prime Minister Ahmed Nazif told parliament that 'the forces of evil and terrorism' were undermining the country's security and that a further extension of the Emergency was required (El-Din 2008b). By ignoring the earlier commitment Nazif sent a message to state officials, police and security officers that they too could act as if rights and freedoms were of little account. One outcome is that security forces believe they can operate with impunity in relation to the population at large.

Culture of abuse

Large numbers of Egyptians testify to increasingly violent treatment at the hands of the police. M.F. was detained in October 1994 at school, where he was a final-year student. Despite eight court orders for his release he was discharged only in May 2002 after spending eight years in four different detention centres, in addition to visits to state security headquarters each time he or his family appealed against detention.

> After my arrest I spent forty-five days at State Security. During the
> first twelve days they interrogated me every day... sometimes they
> interrogated me more than once, always blindfolded, always with my
> hands and feet cuffed together [and with] all kinds of torture – beat-
> ing, whipping, electric shocks to the tips of my fingers and genitalia,
> sometimes to my nipples. I was threatened with rape more than once
> and was kept naked for prolonged periods of time. And even at times
> when there was no physical torture, there was always humiliation and
> insult. I didn't know what they wanted. Their questions didn't make
> any sense, like asking me about what is happening in my village. What
> does that mean? Later in the different detention centres they would
> use electric sticks instead of wires and there were always what they
> call 'reception parties' where we were made to crawl naked on the floor
> while the guards whipped us to move faster.[1]

On his release M.F. tried to start a life. Finding no job opportunities he decided to travel, choosing the country with the cheapest visa,
Sudan. He was stopped at the airport and his passport was confiscated.

To retrieve it he had to check with state security in his governorate and thereby was again subjected to torture and beatings, which cost him the loss of hearing in his left ear. M.F. was detained and tortured like thousands of others rounded up on suspicion of his links with Islamic groups. A list of names or phone numbers found during an illegal search in a suspect's home is usually enough to send the victim on a long journey of horror between State Security and the detention centres. But people like M.F. do not constitute the bulk of torture victims: the majority are ordinary people whose unfortunate paths cross with those of the police. What they have in common is their poverty, their social marginalisation and their lack of contact with 'important' people who could help them out of trouble. The Egyptian Organisation for Human Rights (EOHR) recorded 532 cases of torture between April 1993 and April 2004, of which 120 resulted in death (ICRT 2005). Susan Fayad, director of the El Nadim Center for Psychological Management and Rehabilitation of Victims of Violence, based in Cairo, says that actual numbers are much higher, 'since families usually do not report deaths of their members in fear of harassment from the police' (ICRT 2005). The El Nadim Center observes a huge increase in torture of Egyptians seized by police for petty offences: its caseworkers say that police abuse 'has gone through the roof' (Murphy 2007). Gasser Abdel-Razek of Human Rights Watch observes that in the 1980s torture was applied routinely to members of the political opposition, becoming a standard technique of interrogation; when police officers moved to other posts they took the practice with them. 'It became a culture', he says; 'We have two generations of police who were brought up to use torture against Islamists. But if it's allowed and seen as effective, it spreads' (Murphy 2007). Torture is applied to people, young and old, in towns and villages across the country, as revealed in a host of testimonies to El Nadim:

- A.R. refused to confess to stealing a cow from a neighbouring farm. To force a confession, a police officer soaked him in petrol and set him on fire, resulting in his death a few days later.
- A.T. was killed under torture because he was flirting with a young neighbour whose mother knew a journalist; she in turn knew a police officer, who promised to teach him a lesson.

- A child of 11 was burned on an electric stove in the local police station with the aim of retrieving three packets of tea he was alleged to have stolen from a café in the neighbourhood.
- M.L., a cook, was left with half of his body paralysed because he quit his job at a former minister's house – a breach of Egyptian class ethics for which he was punished with two days of torture in the local police station, during which he was suspended from his wrists while they were tied behind his back.[2]

Police also use torture to solicit confessions from suspects, from members of suspects' families or from neighbours; to complement stories they have obtained from third parties; to force people from their land or homes; or simply to teach respect for authority. Commonly used torture methods include electric shocks, *falaka* (beating the feet), whipping, suspension in painful positions, solitary confinement, rape and sexual abuse, death threats and attacks on relatives. In addition, the El Nadim Center has recently documented several cases of people being drowned or thrown off police buildings.

Special powers

Powers conferred on the authorities under Emergency Law constitute a direct attack on due process and fundamental human rights. Under Article 3, the president can authorise searches and arrests without following provisions of the Criminal Procedures Code; he can also restrict freedom of movement and residence, and impose censorship on all means of communication. Article 3 permits him to widen the scope of these powers through orders such as Decree 4 of 1992, which has been used to prosecute many ordinary Egyptians. Under Article 9 he can transfer individuals accused of crimes under the Penal Code to Emergency State Security Courts and Supreme State Security Courts. These bodies – which are empowered to hear all cases, including those involving people accused of civil crimes – routinely ignore defendants' allegations of torture (FIDH 2005). They often try members of the political opposition, as in the case of forty members of the Muslim Brotherhood who in 2007 received sentences of up to ten years in prison; Amnesty International (2007a) commented that the defendants were all civilians 'tried before a military court where proceedings are notoriously unfair'. It maintains that all such procedures are illegitimate:

> Trying civilians before military courts, whose judges are serving members of the military, flouts international standards of fair trial and is inherently unjust, regardless of whether the defendants are allowed a right of appeal or not. [Amnesty International] has criticized the military trial of the 40 members of the Muslim Brothers. It has attempted three times to send an international observer to the trial but on each occasion the observer was denied access to the military court. (Amnesty International 2007a)

Meanwhile outside the courts the Emergency translates into unlimited and uncensored power exercised by security and state intelligence authorities: in effect the police and other agencies are free to use every form of abuse without restraint.

Mutilation and harassment

When women are involved, torture invariably involves sexual harassment and humiliation. Zeinab is a street vendor selling vegetables in the vicinity of the Helwan metro station near Cairo. She is the head of an extended household which includes her widowed daughter and her two children. Someone who wanted to evict them from the family house had connections to the local police station, where officers ordered a campaign of extreme violence and sexual abuse.

Helwan is famous for its giant iron and steel plant, at which in 1989 workers led one of the most important strikes in recent Egyptian history. It has acquired a new national notoriety in the person of Mohamed al-Sharkawy, a young intelligence officer who led the assault. Zeinab's testimony describes how she met him:

> On the night of mid-Shaaban [a religious occasion for Muslims] we were busy making preparations for a wedding. After midnight the house was surrounded by more than forty armed men, who tried to break into our apartment. My nephew stood up to the officer and asked: 'Where are you going? The women at home are not fully dressed.' The officer pushed him so hard he fell down and they walked in. The girls came out in their nightgowns and the men in their boxer shorts. They beat us all up, not discriminating between men, women or children, and took us. They also wanted to take my sister, an elderly woman, who has brought me up. I covered her body with mine and prevented

them from doing so. I told them she was an elderly woman and cannot walk. They left her, but took the rest of us, eleven people, including women and children, dragged us down the stairs like sheep.

Out on the street, there were four or five minibuses and all the neighbors were standing around on the pavements and on their balconies watching us ... They took me first to El-Zahraa then to Helwan Police Station. They kept us in a smelly and disgustingly filthy room which they called 'the fridge'. The officer asked the informers to urinate in front of us on the floor. The boys were asleep, while I turned my face to the other side out of shame. So they whipped me to force me to look. They stripped me of my clothes and left me naked.

I had three sleepless days and nights. Twice or three times a day they would strip me naked. Mohamed al-Sharkawy said to me, 'You are only good enough for ******* and I'm specialised in ******* .' I pleaded with them: 'Kill me, remove my nails, torture me the way you wish, but don't strip me of my gallabeyya. Even my husband has never seen me fully naked.'

He tied my legs with a thick rope at the ankles and turned me upside down and whipped my soles. In another torture session they stripped me naked again and al-Sharkawy made one of his men lie on top of me. I lost consciousness. They stripped me several times and lay on top of me.

Al-Sharkawy told me: 'I'm going to file a case of prostitution against you. I'll prove I picked you up from a place of ill repute.' And he threatened to would send me down to the prisoners to rape me. He grabbed my breasts and my private parts with his hands. I was naked, while my brother was hanging upside down and his wife lay there naked with a man on top of her.

I was dying. And I was pulling at my body, at my hair, and wanted to die. If they did this to a woman, you can imagine what they did to the men. My nephews saw their own father hanging upside down. They saw him being stripped and electrocuted on his sensitive parts. They saw me and saw their mother naked with men on top of our bodies. Even my brother was made to witness the scene.

My niece was also stripped and whipped. There was another woman with a newborn baby, only four days old. The baby was yellow and was bleeding from the mouth, so they let her go. One of the men was burned, another had both his hands broken, and we're still taking him to doctors [for treatment]. Eleven members of the family have been tortured and scandalised. We can't forgo our rights: reconciliation and compensation are out of the question. It's either they die or we die. (El Nadim Center 2006)

The assault against Zeinab and her family took place in October 2003 and a complaint was soon filed by human rights organisations.

In 2005 her case reached court: there, at a hearing heavily attended by police, al-Sharkawy was found innocent. His colleagues in the courtroom were distributing candy even before the verdict. Children are also victims. According to Human Rights Watch (2004) Egyptian police regularly detain street children they consider 'vulnerable to delinquency' or 'vulnerable to danger'. During arrest these children are routinely beaten with fists and batons and while in custody are subjected to sexual violence, sometimes by adult detainees. They face brutal and humiliating treatment which can be so severe that it constitutes torture. In addition, says the organisation, many men arrested solely for consensual homosexual conduct have been beaten and tortured in police custody. In March 2008, Human Rights Watch and Amnesty International joined in condemnation of sentences imposed on four men accused of 'habitual practice of debauchery', a term used under Egyptian law to prosecute consensual sexual acts between men (Human Rights Watch 2008c). The accused had been seized by police, beaten and subjected to abusive and intrusive physical examinations which were 'medically spurious [and] constitute torture' (Human Rights Watch 2008d).

Media evidence

Zeinab and her family are among the few whose complaints have been heard in public. Most people abused by the police never get to court, their files being closed by the prosecutor general 'for lack of sufficient evidence'. Even when testimonies are available and media provide detailed coverage cases are often closed:

- In May 2005 peaceful demonstrators protesting against a referendum for constitutional change were attacked by police in central Cairo. Women were beaten, stripped and sexually molested in broad daylight and in front of satellite television cameras. The case was closed when the authorities declared they had insufficient evidence to identity the attackers.
- In December 2005 a peaceful sit-in by Sudanese refugees outside offices of the UNHCR was violently dispersed by police, leaving tens of adults and children dead in Mustafa Mahmoud Square, Mohandeseen. This case, currently being processed at the African

Court for Human Rights, was also halted in the public prosecutor's office.

- In October 2004 more than 3,000 people were arrested in the town of 'Arish in Sinai, following a bombing in Taba. Many women were taken hostage and subjected to brutal torture with the aim of locating their husbands and sons. Official statements asserted that just five people had been arrested on charges of planning and carrying out the attacks. The public prosecutor failed to find a case worthy of investigation.

- In March 2005 Nefisa al-Marakbi died as a result of sexual torture following attacks in the village of Sarandu, during which police joined local landowners and thugs in assaulting local people (see Chapter 3). The case was also closed for lack of evidence. (El Nadim Center 2007)

On rare occasions evidence is revealed in court which demonstrates the extremes of brutality common in police stations. In 2006 Emad al-Kabir, a minibus driver from Cairo, was penetrated with a wooden pole by a police sergeant acting on orders from an officer who filmed the assault on his mobile phone and promised to distribute the film to humiliate the victim. The video showed al-Kabir screaming and begging for mercy while being assaulted; when it came into the possession of bloggers it was soon made available to a global audience, with the result that mainstream publications worldwide carried articles expressing outrage at the abuse.[3] Initially the victim was sentenced to three months' imprisonment for 'resisting the authorities'; eventually his abuser received a three-year sentence, though this was not imposed on the officer involved but on the sergeant who had executed the latter's orders. Human Rights Watch (2007a) observed that the case exposed 'a shadowy culture of impunity' in Egyptian police stations.

Denial

The Egyptian government accepts that misconduct does take place. Leading politicians and state officials insist, however, that abuse is associated with only a handful of officers; that allegations are duly investigated; and that, in cases in which abuse is proved, perpetrators receive punishment as dictated by law. In December 2008, Deputy Minister for Legal Affairs Hamid Rashid told the Human Rights Committee at the People's Assembly that over the previous twelve months, 433 complaints of ill conduct had been filed by citizens against policemen, 97 of which were disregarded by the prosecutor's office, which acquitted two policemen and charged five. The remaining complaints, said Rashid, were still under investigation (Abdoun 2008).

He also said the Ministry of the Interior had suspended a total of 280 policemen from duty for violations against citizens and had discharged 1,164 lower-ranking policemen for misconduct and abuse of power (Abdoun 2008). There is ample evidence that ill-treatment including torture is far more widespread than these figures suggest. Torture rooms exist in many police stations, equipped with instruments of abuse financed not by the salaries of individual police or state security officers but by the ministry itself (the budget of which is higher than the combined allocations for the ministries of education and health). The state itself has made abuse integral to the regime of control.

Although Egypt's constitution proscribes torture and ill treatment, the law facilitates abuse. According to Article 42:

> Any citizen arrested, detained or whose freedom is restricted shall be treated in a manner concomitant with the preservation of his dignity. No physical or moral harm is to be inflicted upon him. He may not be detained or imprisoned except in places defined by laws organizing prisons. If a confession is proved to have been made by a person under any of the aforementioned forms of duress or coercion, it shall be considered invalid and futile.

Consistent with this approach, in 1986 the government ratified without reservation the Convention against Torture and Other Cruel, Inhuman or Degrading Treatment or Punishment, publishing this information in 1988 in *Al-Waqa'e Al-Misreya* (the official gazette). The Convention includes a precise definition of torture:

> Any act by which severe pain or suffering, whether physical or mental, is intentionally inflicted on a person for such purposes as obtaining from him or a third person information or a confession, punishing him for an act he or a third person has committed or is suspected of having committed, or intimidating or coercing him or a third person, or for any reason based on discrimination of any kind, when such pain or suffering is inflicted by or at the instigation of or with the consent or acquiescence of a public official or other person acting in an official capacity.[4]

Egypt's Penal Code suggests a different approach, however. Article 126 notes that 'Any government employee or official who instructs others to torture, or himself carries out the torture of an accused to get confessions shall be sentenced to three to ten years' hard labour in jail, and if a torture victim is killed the torturer shall be punished by the same sentence of intentional murder.' Here the law recognises torture only if the victim is accused of a specific crime and if the practice is used to extract a confession: if no confession is targeted and if the victim is not accused of crimes, abuse is not defined as torture.

The Egyptian government has not signed the Optional Protocol for the Convention against Torture, which regulates monitoring of states' behaviour by means of visits undertaken by independent international and national bodies; nor has the United Nations Special Rapporteur on Torture been able to visit Egypt. The Rapporteur may solicit an invitation based on factors such as the number, credibility and gravity of allegations received. Despite numerous attempts to arrange visits to Egypt, on each occasion the United Nations has been rebuffed by the government. Among 139 states that are parties to the Convention against Torture, Egypt is one of only five against which the United Nations Committee against Torture has launched a special investigation into allegations of systematic abuse.

In 2003 lawyers and human rights activists formed the Egyptian Association Against Torture (EAAT 2003).[5] This was denied official registration under Article 11 of the association law, which prevents non-governmental organisations engaging in 'political activities'. The association nonetheless issued a report, *Fifty Days' Harvest of Citizens' Rights*, documenting torture incidents during the fifty days of the conference held in 2005 by the ruling NDP. This recorded the torture of ninety citizens, seven of whom died in police stations and State Security centres. In a further report on people who died under torture or as a result of torture between May 2004 and May 2005 EAAT identified twenty-six fatalities (EAAT 2005). It commented that these represented 'only the tip of the iceberg', adding that collection of firm evidence was made increasingly difficult by the danger that ill-treatment would be revisited upon those who testified to their experiences: 'Living under the confines of a strongly oppressive rule, like that of Egypt, where perpetrators of torture are given unlimited authority, any victim who complains or tries to publicize his or her case, subject[s] themselves to great risk' (EAAT 2005).

In the face of overwhelming evidence of torture, leading politicians and state officials have maintained a policy of denial and/or attacked their accusers for defaming Egypt. Halawi (2005) describes 'relentless campaigns' against human rights organisations accused of being 'agents of the West ... portrayed as recipients of foreign funding, keen to tarnish their government's reputation, and subject to the dictates of the West in general, and the US in particular'. Officials have also attacked the media: in an interview with the daily newspaper *Al-Misry Al-Yawm* in 2007, the official spokesman of the Ministry of Interior, General Ahmed Diaa al-Din, accused independent newspapers that reported torture of adopting 'an agitational methodology'. In a revealing statement, he added: 'I am not referring to a particular newspaper. This is an "aggressive" campaign that targets the achievement of certain objectives and the prevalence of torture during the last months did not go beyond five in a thousand' (ANHRI 2007). The Arabic Network for Human Rights Information (ANHRI) commented that this was a significant admission: 'It is a confession that denies previous allegations by the Ministry of Interior that torture does not go beyond individual malpractices.' The organisation continued:

> [W]hy does the assistant to the Minister of Interior consider publishing on crimes of torture an act of agitation? And who is the target population for this agitation? Is it Egyptian public opinion, who from the point of view of the Ministry of Interior, should not know about what is happening in police stations and state security headquarters? Or is it the victims of torture themselves who in his opinion do not deserve to share their pains and humiliation by the police... Does the assistant to the Minister of Interior wish the press to be silent so that his officers might torture in peace?
>
> And our question is: five in 1,000 what? Does he mean five in 1,000 of the Egyptian population suffer torture? Or that five in 1,000 of Egyptian police commit the crime of torture? Or that five in 1,0000 citizens who visit police stations are subject to torture? (ANHRI 2007)

How did we get here?

Those most often subjected to violence are the poor and the marginalised, but the state also targets journalists, activists, judges and even members of parliament. In March 2003, police assaulted and arrested two MPs, Hamdeen Sabahi and Mohamed Farid Hassanein, who were participating in a protest against the invasion of Iraq. Sabahi, who represents the nationalist Karama Party, recounted his experience:

> [I was] suddenly pounced on by 10 plainclothes police agents who attacked me with sticks and truncheons. A few protestors came to rescue me, and a man and his wife managed to get me into their car and drive me to the Bar Association. While I was standing outside the syndicate, I was attacked again, this time by nearly 40 plainclothes police officers. They dragged me to the sidewalk on the other side of the street and kept beating me. (El Din 2003)

Sabahi later accused the police of 'a series of grave offences in breach of the constitution, the law, human rights covenants and the trust of the Egyptian people in general' (El Din 2003).

In the 1990s the main target of police brutality was the Islamist movement. Thousands were detained and tortured and dozens were killed extrajudicially by state authorities unconcerned about the process of law. The regime claimed to be pursuing a national war on terror, which it said had been initiated in 1981 when Islamist army officer Khalid al-Islambuli assassinated President Sadat. Later terrorist attacks – notably the Luxor murders of 1997, which claimed the lives of many tourists – fed the state's conviction that it need not follow formal legal procedures. During the 1990s television broadcasts often carried pictures of police officers killed in confrontations which involved wholesale attacks on villages or urban quarters. Police were described as martyrs and the Egyptian public was led to believe that civilians who died deserved their fate. State Security became an authority in its own right, often boasting that it had become the highest authority in the land. For almost ten years police brutality spread uncontrolled, allowing perpetrators to believe that their behaviour was approved of and encouraging others to emulate them.

In 1992 Human Rights Watch produced an extensive report on torture and detention in Egypt. *Behind Closed Doors* identified a major problem of denial on the part of state authorities, which routinely characterised victims of abuse in ways designed to discredit them. According to ministers the state was dealing with 'fanatics who use violence'; complaints about their treatment, said officials, invariably came from 'members of extremist groups' (Human Rights Watch 1992: 126). Human Rights Watch observed that victims' alleged political affiliations were irrelevant: the abuse violated a host of international norms and could not be justified. It added that there was already a mass of evidence to show that 'security dragnets' were cast so wide that all manner of people were detained and abused, often tortured for information they did not possess (Human Rights Watch 1992: 128). A number of international organisations challenged the Egyptian state on its record; so too the US State Department, which noted formally both that detainees were tortured and that perpetrators escaped without challenge (Human Rights Watch 1992: 166, 171). At the same time the USA increased economic and military support for the regime, insisting disingenuously that Egypt's armed forces had not been linked to the abuses (Human Rights Watch 1992: 171).

The USA and the Egyptian state have since entered a collaboration in which each seeks to profit from systematic practice of torture. Following the 11 September attacks and President Bush's declaration of a global 'war on terror', the Egyptian regime became part of a network of transportation, incarceration and torture – the 'extraordinary rendition' of prisoners held by US authorities. According to Mayer (2005), rendition had been under way since 1995, when American agents had approached the Mubarak government to propose the arrangement and 'Egypt embraced the idea'. Many prisoners were subsequently transported secretly to detention centres at which practices included extremes of abuse: prisoners were stripped and blindfolded; suspended from ceilings or doorframes with feet just touching the floor; beaten with fists, whips, metal rods or other objects; subjected to electric shocks; doused with cold water; and sexually assaulted. The partnership between American and Egyptian security agencies was said to be 'extraordinarily close': Mayer quotes one American security agent to the effect that Egyptian interrogators were able within hours to obtain answers to questions provided by their counterparts (Mayer 2005).

Some prisoners did not survive: according to former CIA official Robert Barr, 'If you want a serious interrogation, you send a prisoner to Jordan. If you want them to be tortured, you send them to Syria. If you want someone to disappear – never to see them again – you send them to Egypt.'[6] Human Rights Watch has compiled a special report on rendition to Egypt. It observed that the practice has taken place without due process such as extradition hearings before judicial authorities:

Once in Egypt, most of the rendered individuals were held in prolonged incommunicado detentions and in several cases were 'disappeared'- that is, the government refused to acknowledge their whereabouts or even the fact that they were in its custody. In the handful of cases in which information eventually does surface, it turns out that the suspects have been tortured or otherwise severely mistreated. For the rest, nothing is known, and it is reasonable to fear that they too have been subjected to torture and ill-treatment. (Human Rights Watch 2004)

Falk (2002: 112) comments on the implications of this policy and its further endorsement since the events of 11 September. A series of states worldwide, he suggests, have taken up a 'hunting licence' offered by the USA, imitating and generalising American methods. Abuse of prisoners in Iraq, Afghanistan and Guantánamo Bay is seen as further encouragement for 'an unconditional authorization for state violence' (Falk 2003: 112). It is in this context that the Nadim Center in Cairo notes widespread use of electric shocks administered to victims held in what Egyptian police refer to as the 'Abu Ghraib' position, whereby wires are connected to the genitals and the nipples (El Nadim Center 2007). Gamal Taj El-Deen Hassan of the Sawasya Human Rights and Anti-Discrimination Centre, also reports that torturers in Egypt 'seem now to compare their methods to what happened in Iraq and say "hey, there are more things that we need to try". And now they try the most horrendous kinds of torture' (Mekay 2004).

But even these extreme forms of abuse have not been viewed as torture in the USA, where officials maintained throughout the years of the Bush administration that they were merely specific forms of interrogation. Elisa Massimino, Washington director of Human Rights First, has observed that many governments hide behind the Americans: 'in, say, Egypt, the Egyptians will say "What are you going to do? The U.S. says this isn't torture".'[7] Confident in the largely uncritical support of US administrations for its domestic security policy, the Mubarak regime has continued to use American denial as an alibi for its own malpractice.

Who is responsible?

Until recently Egyptian human rights organisations were reluctant to identify specific political authorities as responsible for torture. During the 1990s their statements, press releases and advocacy materials named individual officers, police stations or detention centres as implicated in abuse – but did not link them directly with those who occupy high political office. Since the beginning of the new millennium, however, and with the emergence of street protests – first in solidarity with the Palestinian intifada, then against the war on Iraq and in demand of decent living conditions – Egypt has witnessed an upsurge of protest that cuts across society, involving workers, peasants, government employees, physicians, teachers and others. According to Gasser Abdel-Razak of Human Rights Watch, 'We've seen dissent spreading beyond those who are politically organized, for instance [those involved in] the labor unrest; so the regime feels it needs to make its people afraid to control its fate' (Murphy 2007).

When in 2003 lawyers and human rights activists formed EAAT, they argued that abuse could not be explained by the sadistic behaviour of individuals or even groups of police but was part of a coherent strategy:

> When we talk about torture in Egypt we are not talking about a violation here or there. Nor are we talking about the sadism of a number of Egyptian police officers who enjoy to watch [*sic*] the suffering of others. When we talk about torture in Egypt we are talking about an oppressive policy that is adopted by the Ministry of Interior and security bodies and authorities, an organized, systematic and ongoing policy used against citizens.
>
> Egyptian authorities use torture as a systematic and organized tool to terrorize citizens and to ensure complete submission of the people to the policies of those authorities. (EAAT 2003)

EAAT concluded that use of torture is 'a conscious and wilfull choice of a policy'.

Increasingly often protestors demand that senior political figures should answer for the conduct of institutions over which they enjoy authority. Following the assault on democracy activists in Cairo in May 2005, campaigners demanded the resignation of the minister of the interior, General Habib al-Adly.[8] The Egyptian Initiative for Personal Rights has since observed that, as chairman of the Supreme Police Council, '[President] Mubarak could easily be held personally responsible for the atmosphere of impunity that allows torture to persist and kill more citizens every year'.[9] Its director, Hossam Bahgat, comments that in the 2005 elections the government made great play of its commitment to constitutional and political reform: 'Yet one cannot help but notice the conspicuous absence in Mubarak's re-election platform of what many would agree is Egypt's number one human rights problem: the prevalence of torture and ill-treatment of citizens in police stations and other places of detention all over the country' (Bahgat 2005). The Egyptian human rights movement has produced ample documentation on torture, says Bahgat, having been persistent in reporting incidents and calling on the government to intervene. Notwithstanding pressure within Egypt and from abroad, the practice has continued unabated, giving Egypt 'one of the worst records in the world when it comes to torture' (Bahgat 2005).

In August 2007, eighteen organizations, political groups and trade-union committees issued a public statement holding the president to account:

> A number of citizens have entered police stations alive and have left in coffins to their graves, victims of the brutality and criminality of Egyptian police. Each time the Ministry of Interior issued a statement that twists the truths, reflects complicity with torturers and sometimes even rewards them...
>
> Are those crimes the responsibility of the Minister of Interior alone? Doesn't the president, who is the chair of the higher council of the police and the chair of the higher council of the judiciary etc., bear the prime responsibility of that moral and legal degradation of the police institution? Is it still possible for anybody to claim that this barbarity is merely the result of 'individual' practices?...
>
> We the undersigned organizations hold the President of the Republic responsible for torture and killing in police stations.[10]

Demanding an apology from the head of state, independent investigations into torture allegations, and immediate measures to stop abuse, the signatories committed to a continuing campaign 'to highlight the crimes of torture committed in Egypt, its perpetrators, those who order it and those who are complicit with it', concluding: 'We shall have our files ready ... when the time comes for accountability and justice.'[11]

8

Mubarak
in the international arena

Anne Alexander

What is the effect of Egypt's relationship with the USA on the Mubarak regime? Is it an asset or liability for the regime and how does it affect prospects for 'regime change from below'? American financial and military support for Egypt has been an important factor in the current regime's longevity: US funding subsidises the coercive apparatus of the state and US aid enriches bureaucrats and business-men close to the regime, as do economic policies promoted by the USA in Egypt. The nature of its engagement with the USA, however, also increases the Mubarak regime's vulnerability. There is a risk that the alliance will create 'feedback' mechanisms, stimulating popular mobilisation in opposition to the regime's domestic policies, together with protests over its external relations. Such interactions can play a dynamic role in enabling movements that seek radical change. Between 1945 and 1952, rising levels of socio-economic discontent in Egypt, together with popular anger at the Arab defeat in Palestine in 1948 and the Egyptian government's long-term dependence on Britain, intersected to generate a mass movement which fatally undermined the monarchy (Alexander 2007). This chapter examines the contradic-tory relationship between Mubarak and his allies in Washington, and its impact on relations with other Arab states and on Egypt's neighbours, the Palestinians.

Reactions to the killing of Egyptian president Anwar al-Sadat in 1981 illustrate starkly contrasting views on policies with which he was most closely identified – those of *infitah* and peace with Israel, America's most-favoured ally. Four US presidents – Richard Nixon, Gerald Ford, Jimmy Carter and Ronald Reagan – were among the many international political leaders who attended Sadat's funeral. But in contrast to the vast crowds which accompanied Nasser's funeral cortège in 1970, the streets remained empty as Sadat was laid to rest. While eulogies for their Nobel prizewinning leader filled the international press, many ordinary Egyptians enjoyed surreptitious celebrations.

Sadat's strategic and economic opening to the West, initiated in the mid-1970s, had complex aims. Egypt's economic relationship with the Soviet Union and its allies, established in the 1950s, had been causing increasing difficulty. Barter-exchange agreements with states of the Eastern bloc had been a key part of Nasser's economic policy, providing for export of primary commodities such as cotton, rice and phosphates, and servicing large debts which Egypt had accumulated through the purchase of Soviet arms. But a growing need for food imports from the USA, Australia, Canada and Europe, which could only be paid for in convertible currency, compelled Sadat to seek new external links (Waterbury 1985). As he looked to an alliance with the USA, Sadat also hoped to weaken his opponents in the Egyptian military and in the ruling party, the Arab Socialist Union, among whom several were keen advocates of the relationship with Moscow.

Sadat's first move was to launch the October War of 1973, during which the Egyptian army crossed the Suez Canal, temporarily throwing back Israeli forces. It rapidly became clear, however, that far from being a move to claim Nasser's mantle, the war was an attempt to improve Egypt's negotiating position in American-sponsored peace talks with Israel. The first signs of realignment came in 1974 with declaration of *infitah* – an economic opening to the West. One of the consequences was the 'intifada of bread' of January 1977, a popular uprising in protest at removal of subsidies on basic goods demanded by the IMF (see Chapter 1). Although Sadat was forced to restore the subsidies, he also hastened to establish full relations with the West – a key means by which he could guarantee food imports and restrain popular anger. Later the same year he flew to Jerusalem, appearing before the Israeli parliament to call for a negotiated peace. A bilateral peace treaty was signed in March 1979, withdrawing Egypt from the Arab–Israeli conflict and establishing a new relationship with the USA, which was soon supplying unprecedentedly large sums of aid and military grants and loans.

Aid and arms

By any standards the flow of aid and arms from the USA to Egypt since has been astounding. Between 1977 and 2007 the Egyptian government received almost $62 billion dollars from the United States in economic aid and foreign military assistance, an average of $2.1 billion per year.[1] Only one other state has regularly received more than Egypt: its neighbour and sometime enemy, Israel. Egypt's budget from Washington's Economic Support Fund (ESF) for the financial year 2008 was larger than that of the whole of sub-Saharan Africa, despite a significant decrease in US transfers to Egypt since 1998 (US Government 2007: 94–5). In 2008, only Afghanistan received more than Egypt from the regular ESF budget. US military assistance to Egypt also dwarfs that to any other state except Israel. Washington's 2008 budget for Foreign Military Financing promised US$2.4 billion to Israel and US$1.3 billion to Egypt. By comparison, the next largest requests were for Pakistan at a mere $3 million and Jordan at $2 million (US Government 2007: 98).

Egypt has received numerous large transfers of advanced military equipment. A typical deal announced in 1999 involved hardware worth almost $4 billion, including fighter jets, helicopters, missiles and hundreds of tanks. Pentagon officials said the equipment would support US foreign policy and national security goals, Egypt being 'a friendly country that has always been, and will remain, an important power for political stability and economic progress in the Middle East' (Ibrahim 1999). Such support is all the more remarkable given that Egypt is rarely involved in military conflicts with external powers. With the single exception of a minor role in the Gulf War of 1991, Egyptian troops have not been in action since 1973; they nonetheless play an important role in supporting American policy in both the Middle East and Africa. As the US State Department notes approvingly, Egypt provides military assistance and training to a number of African states in order 'to bolster stability and moderation in the region' (US State Department 2008). Meanwhile joint exercises such as the biennial Operation Bright Star, initiated in 1981, are the largest combined military manoeuvres in the Middle East. By 2001 Bright Star involved 70,000 troops, among whom 23,000 came from the USA (Ibrahim 2007). According to the Egyptian general in charge of the 2007 exercise, it provided 'an opportunity to get acquainted with each other's equipment, tactics and training. The exercise is designed to improve readiness and interoperability and to strengthen relationships between Egypt, the US and other participating forces' (Ibrahim 2007).

Liberalisation

For thirty years American officials have sought to reshape Egyptian economic affairs. Formally, they have encouraged successive regimes to conform with market principles. As Mitchell (2002: 236) observes, this long campaign has been largely rhetorical in character, as a formal commitment to market mechanisms has been accompanied by determined efforts to entrench American interests as key beneficiaries of reform. In the 1980s Egypt was required to reduce tariffs on agricultural imports and to open the state sector to foreign investors; meanwhile wheat provided under the American 'Food for Peace' programme exacerbated Egypt's dependence on imported food and allowed US firms to dominate the Egyptian market to the exclusion of European competitors (Dethier and Funk, 1987: 24). US weapons manufacturers and giant corporations such as General Electric, Westinghouse and Bechtel profited from the aid regime: Mitchell (2002: 238) suggests that between 1974 and 1991, almost 60 per cent of American economic assistance to Egypt was spent in the USA and that much of the rest went to US corporations and institutions operating in Egypt. Springborg (1989: 107) notes that American aid also contributed to militarisation of the Egyptian economy by providing funds used by the military industrial sector to diversify into areas such as production of food and consumer goods. US grain shipments under Public Law 480 ('Food for Peace') have dwindled but Egypt is still one of the largest markets worldwide for American wheat – and the USA has recently been Egypt's largest bilateral trading partner, with Egyptian exports growing from $79.1 million dollars in 1985 to almost $2.4 billion in 2007 (US Census Bureau 2008).[2] The interaction between US strategic and economic interests is the most important factor shaping American intervention in the Egyptian economy, as the example of the Qualifying Industrial Zones (QIZ) agreement of 2004 illustrates. Despite intense lobbying efforts by Egypt, the US government has been reluctant to sign a bilateral free-trade agreement. Instead, under the QIZ scheme, an extension of the US–Israeli Free Trade Agreement, Egyptian goods manufactured in a QIZ can enter the USA duty-free, provided they contain at least 10.5 per cent input from Israel.[3] Yadav (2007) argues that the QIZ agreement has different meanings for the three parties: the Egyptian government views it as protecting the textile industry and as a stepping-stone to a bilateral trade agreement with the USA, whereas the scheme is primarily of political importance to Israel and the USA. It was viewed by the Bush administration as part of a broader political strategy – creation of a Middle East that 'trades in freedom' – while on the Israeli side, it has been largely about 'removing the Arab "taboo" of doing business with Israel in the open' and reviving the process of 'normalisation' of economic relations (Yadav 2007). Here Egypt's weak position in the world market, rather than its status as a recipient of US aid, is the lever by which US policy objectives are achieved.

Egypt and the Palestinians

For over thirty years Egypt has played a central role in US policy towards the Israeli–Palestinian conflict. American officials hoped that the Camp David Accords of 1978, which preceded Sadat's agreement with Israel, would pave the way for a series of bilateral treaties between Israel and other Arab states. They intended that a mix of economic incentives and military threats, similar to those deployed in discussions with Sadat, would persuade Arab governments to abandon the Palestinians of the Occupied Territories to a future under Israeli rule while they also absorbed the millions of Palestinian refugees who fled Israeli forces in 1948 and 1967. An equally important motive, in the bipolar world of the late 1970s, was exclusion of the Soviet Union from any role in an Arab–Israeli 'peace' process.

Achieving the second goal proved easier than the first, as the collapse of the Eastern bloc left the USA without rivals in the Middle East. Although Yasir Arafat of the PLO and King Hussein of Jordan eventually followed in Sadat's footsteps to embrace Israeli leaders on the White House lawn, there has been no peace agreement – largely because terms on offer from Israel and the USA have implied a Palestinian surrender (Said 1994; Chomsky 1999). While resistance within the Occupied Territories has been one stumbling block to outright capitulation by the Arab states, a further important factor is the question of the refugees. In 2007 Egypt was home to only 50,000 Palestinians, in comparison to the 400,000 living in Lebanon, 460,000 in Syria and 1.8 million in Jordan (IRIN 2007). The costs of abandoning support for Palestinian claims to return to their former homes are much higher for Israel's other Arab neighbours than they were for Sadat.

The intractability of the Middle East conflict has nonetheless had profound implications for the Mubarak regime. It has preserved Egypt's strategic value to the USA, not only as an example for other Arab states to follow but also as a mediator in disputes between Palestinian factions and as an enforcer of US and Israeli policies. Repeated Israeli military attacks on other Arab states, particularly Lebanon, coupled with widespread popular support across the Arab world for the Palestinian resistance, have made it difficult for Egypt's rulers to achieve full 'normalisation' in relations with Israel. Popular solidarity with the Palestinian intifada has also been a factor in the Mubarak regime's internal crisis (see Chapter 5).

'Normalisation'

For the Palestinian national movement the short-term effects of the 1979 Egyptian–Israeli peace treaty were catastrophic. As Chomsky (1999) notes, peace in Sinai meant war for Lebanon. Israeli forces invaded Lebanon in 1978 (only months after Sadat's much heralded visit to Jerusalem) and again in 1982, when in the wake of the PLO's retreat from Beirut thousands of Palestinian civilians were massacred in the Sabra and Shatila refugee camps by Israel's Lebanese allies (Chomsky 1999: 67, Fisk 1990). Meanwhile, the rise to power in Israel of the right-wing Likud heralded a new phase of aggressive settlement expansion in the Occupied Territories. Mubarak's reaction to the invasion of 1982 was to halt moves towards 'normalisation' by recalling the Egyptian ambassador. Despite fury in the Arab world over the invasion and the massacres, he did not withdraw from the peace treaty: such action would have jeopardised the new relationship with the USA. Instead Egypt–Israel relations lapsed into a state of 'cold peace' (Beinin 1985), undisturbed by the heightened levels of resistance which began with the Palestinian intifada of 1987.

Sadat's peace treaty was punished – at least formally – when other members of the Arab League suspended Egypt and moved the organisation's headquarters from Cairo to Tunis. By the late 1980s, however, Egypt was being rehabilitated, largely as a result of a realignment of regional forces prompted by the Iran–Iraq war. Egyptian arms and Saudi money were two crucial links in the network of support behind Iraq as Saddam Hussein took on the Islamic Republic. Ironically, it was Saddam Hussein's defeat by the USA in the Gulf War of 1991 which provided opportunities for revitalisation of Egypt's ambitions to regional leadership: Mubarak played a central role, at Washington's request, in bringing together Arab participants in Operation Desert Storm, which expelled Iraqi forces from Kuwait. Even Hafez al-Assad of Syria, who had little cause to love either Mubarak or the USA, sent troops. US officials promptly wrote off some $7 billion of Egypt's military debt (Habeeb 2002: 100).

Within two years of the Gulf War, secret talks between Israeli and Palestinian negotiators in the Norwegian capital Oslo appeared to have brought about a dramatic breakthrough. PLO Chairman Yasir Arafat and Israeli Prime Minister Yitzhak Rabin met at the White House while a beaming US President Bill Clinton looked on. The Declaration of Principles of September 1993 set in motion a seven-year process of negotiations. This gained for the PLO the trappings of statehood in fragments of the Occupied Territories, but there was no agreement on key 'final status' issues and Israel maintained control over the borders of a Palestinian shadow state.

Egypt had been initially sidelined by the Oslo Accords but was quickly drawn in by the USA as a key player. In May 1994, Rabin and Arafat signed an agreement in Cairo providing for Israeli concessions in the Gaza Strip and Jericho and the creation of the Palestinian Authority (PA). With the signing of a Jordan–Israel peace treaty later the same year, Egypt's isolation as the only Arab state to have made peace with Israel was at an end. The language of the Cairo Agreement pointed to future cooperation between Israeli and Palestinian officials 'on the one hand' and Egypt and Jordan 'on the other'.[4] Gaza and the West Bank would be Israel's gateways to the Arab world, with 'normalisation' legitimised by the presence of Palestinian policemen. At the height of the Oslo process Egypt facilitated negotiations, pushing the PLO into a set of triangular relationships with the USA and Israel which were a mirror of its own unequal alliances. As the process began to break down, Egypt's role became more direct, Mubarak and his officials acting as a channel for US and Israeli pressure on the PA through the mechanism of security cooperation. When a new intifada erupted in September 2000, Israel's grip on the Occupied Territories was tighter than ever.

Egypt and the rise of Hamas

From 2002 onwards Egyptian officials began to play an active role in two key areas of Palestinian politics. First they continued to transmit US and Israeli pressure to the PA, particularly by means of influence on a reformed Palestinian security apparatus. The Egyptians claimed to be acting as impartial mediators between Palestinian factions, hosting talks between Fatah and the Islamists of Hamas, and brokering ceasefires when in 2007 the two factions came into conflict (Kershner and El-Khodary 2007). Meanwhile Mubarak dealt directly with the Israeli government, facilitating the latter's strategy of 'disengagement' from Gaza. Under plans agreed with Israeli Prime Minister Sharon, Egyptian security advisers were to police the Palestinian security services after Sharon had organised evacuation of Israeli settlements. A joint statement by the Palestinian factions in June 2004 condemned Egypt's role as 'part of a policy of deception and fraud whose goal is to imprison the Palestinian people in a giant jail in Gaza while controlling the sea, the air and the borders and simultaneously widening the occupation in the West Bank with settlements and the separation fence' (Regular 2004). Egyptian officials countered that security advisers would only go to Gaza with a clear invitation from the PA. During 2005, Egypt appeared to be steering the PA (now under Arafat's successor Mahmoud Abbas) towards accepting an expanded Egyptian security role in the Gaza Strip. By August 2005 Egyptian security officials were training 5,000 Palestinian policemen in the Gaza Strip in preparation for Israeli withdrawal. Meanwhile, progress towards Egyptian–Israeli normalisation resumed with the return of the Egyptian ambassador to Tel Aviv and the signing of a $2.5 billion deal for the sale to Israel of Egyptian natural gas, which later caused uproar among the Egyptian opposition. In September 2005 Israeli settlements in Gaza were dismantled and Israeli troops withdrew from the area. Under the terms of an agreement brokered by the USA, the Rafah crossing between Gaza and Egypt was to be under joint Palestinian and Egyptian control, but overseen by a European monitoring force.

This neat division of responsibility between Fatah, Egypt and Israel was upset by Palestinian voters, who in January 2006 returned a majority of Hamas representatives in elections to the Palestinian Legislative Council. A new Palestinian government under Ismail Haniyeh soon faced an ultimatum from the Middle East Quartet (the United Nations, the USA, Russia and the European Union), the major financial sponsors of the PA. Hamas, they insisted, must commit to 'non-violence' and to recognition of Israel, or forfeit all aid. In the absence of such guarantees, in April 2006 the USA and EU withdrew all support to the PA, adding to intense pressure on the population of Gaza produced by an Israeli blockade and chronic food shortages (United Nations 2006). Two months later Israel reinvaded Gaza – but failed to crush Hamas.

The US officials now turned to Fatah, with Egyptian support, to achieve what the Israeli army had been unable to achieve. Egypt was to play a key role in preparing Fatah's militiamen for civil war, with the aim of destroying the Palestinian Islamists. In December 2006 Abbas called for new elections and dissolution of the Hamas government. Meanwhile Egyptian arms began to flow across the border to Fatah-controlled PA security services; one shipment in December 2006 included 2,000 AK-47 rifles, 20,000 magazines and 2 million rounds of ammunition (Harel and Issacharoff 2006). Fatah security forces also received training in Egypt. In June 2007, however, Hamas routed Fatah's forces and seized military control of Gaza, pre-empting a US-backed military coup organised by Muhammad Dahlan, former head of the PA's Preventative Security Service (Rose 2008). One factor prompting the Hamas initiative was a report in the Israeli newspaper *Ha'aretz* that Abbas had asked Israel to allow passage to a further arms shipment from Egypt, including 'dozens of armored cars, hundreds of armor-piercing RPG rockets, thousands of hand grenades and millions of rounds of ammunition' (Harel and Issacharoff 2007).

Fatah's humiliation in Gaza contributed to worsening relations between Israel and Egypt. Israeli officials accused Mubarak of turning a blind eye to arms smuggling to Hamas and increased their pressure on the USA to block or reduce aid to Egypt (Sharp 2008). Mubarak was now facing an acute dilemma, which came to a head in January 2008. Israel had tightened its siege on Gaza, periodically cutting off electricity supplies, blockading almost all goods and causing immense suffering to the civilian population. On 22 January, Palestinian women demonstrated in Rafah, calling on Egyptian forces to open the border. A series of explosions breached the border fence and soon hundreds of thousands of Palestinians were pouring through into Egyptian territory. Publicly the Egyptian government welcomed the Palestinians, laying the blame for their plight on Israel's policy of blockade. At the same time it ordered suppression of demonstrations in Cairo. Some 1,000 people, mostly members of the Muslim Brotherhood, were arrested on 24 January as they attempted to gather in support of the Palestinians (BBC 2008a). Mubarak was eventually compelled to begin direct negotiations with Hamas over policing of the border.

In December 2008, when Israel again assaulted Gaza, and Egypt refused to permit its residents to escape by entering Egypt, Mubarak was widely accused of having collaborated with the Palestinians' tormentors. Mass media across the region noted the visit of Israeli Foreign Minister Tzipi Livni to Cairo a day before the attacks on Gaza, suggesting that Mubarak had known in advance of the assault. From Lebanon, Hezbollah leader Hassan Nasrallah broadcast live on Arabic-language satellite channels, declaring cryptically: 'I am not calling for a coup in Egypt ... but if you [the Egyptian government] do not open the Rafah crossing, if you do not help the Palestinian people, you will be considered accomplices in the massacre and the blockade' (Saleh 2008). In an unusual step Egyptian security services permitted a number of closely controlled demonstrations in central Cairo, although protests which began in universities and in provincial centres were attacked and many activists arrested (see Chapter 1).

'War on terror'

It has often been assumed that, as with economic policy, Sadat's turn to the West implied a comprehensive change in Egypt's political system. On this view alliance with the USA prompted Sadat to abandon the authoritarian populism of the Nasser era, with its corporatist institutions of political control such as the National Union (later the Arab Socialist Union [ASU]), opting instead for multiparty democracy. Triumphalist rhetoric emanating from Washington about a worldwide democratic revolution is hard to square with the reality of authoritarian rule in many states closely allied to the USA. As Anderson correctly charges, US foreign policy has often been an obstacle to genuine political transformation; collusion with 'autocratic and compliant friends ... permitting fixed elections and human rights fakery ... that allow it [the USA] and its client regimes to continue in the game' (Kassem 2004: 3).

The economic liberalisation of the 1990s has not been matched by a similar process of political reform. Successive US administrations, Republican and Democrat, have decided over the past three decades that their long-term interests are best served by maintaining Mubarak in power, even if he shows scant respect for civil liberties. Despite systematic violations of human rights, rigged elections and evidence of a persistent culture of torture (see Chapter 7), US aid has continued to flow. Under the banner of the 'war on terror', American policy has become even more intimately connected with the most repressive parts of Mubarak's regime, notably through Egypt's integration into a global network of subcontracted torturers run under the CIA's Extraordinary Rendition programme (Popham and Taylor 2007). This partnership builds on a long history of US–Egyptian intelligence cooperation, which has also provided valuable support for US military intervention elsewhere in the region, such as US operations in Afghanistan. A bare two weeks after hijacked airliners crashed into the World Trade Center and the Pentagon on 11 September 2001, US Secretary of State Colin Powell praised Egypt's role in dealing with 'the scourge of terrorism', adding:

> Egypt, as all of us know, is really ahead of us on this issue. They [*sic*] have had to deal with acts of terrorism in recent years in the course of their history. And we have much to learn from them and there is much we can do together. (Powell 2001)

Invasion of Iraq by the USA in 2003 presented many dangers to the Egyptian regime. Mubarak was unable to reprise his 1991 role of rallying the support of other Arab states for a UN-sponsored but US-led military campaign. The war was deeply unpopular in Egypt, triggering the bitterest street demonstrations for a generation (see Chapter 5). It may also have intensified Mubarak's determination not to concede democratic reform – and in particular not to concede political space to the Islamists who dominate opposition movements.

The history of the Egyptian Islamist movement demonstrates another set of dilemmas for both the USA and the Egyptian regime. Both the actions of the Egyptian state and US global strategy played an important role in the radicalisation of a generation of Islamists who abandoned attempts to change society by persuasion and pious example in favour conducting a global *jihad* through 'the propaganda of the deed'. In the 1980s many of the same Islamist activists, released from detention after Sadat's assassination, made their way to Afghanistan. Here, transformed by US State Department rhetoric from 'terrorists' into 'freedom fighters', they fought a *jihad* against the Soviet Union, funded and armed by the USA and Saudi Arabia. One of those to make the journey was Ayman al-Zawahiri, arrested and jailed in the aftermath of Sadat's assassination, and later Osama bin Laden's chief collaborator. Other Egyptians said to have a played a key role in the establishment and/or development of al-Qaeda include Subhi Abu Sitta, Ali Amin al-Rashidi Mustafa, Abu al-Yazid and Yusif al-Dardiri (Ashour 2008). According to Ashour, activists of the Egyptian Jihad group 'were the co-founders and the main administrators behind the establishment of al-Qaeda' (Ashour 2008).

Thousands of 'Arab Afghans' had earlier taken *jihad* back to Egypt. During the 1990s, the Islamic Groups (Gama'at Islamiyya), Al-Jihad and its offshoot Vanguards of Conquest claimed to have assassinated scores of government officials, military personnel, foreign tourists and Egyptian civilians (see Chapter 6). The Egyptian authorities used the draconian Emergency Law, providing for suspects to be held in 'preventative detention' without charge and to be brought before military courts, which subsequently tried thousands of defendants. By the turn of the new century, the radical Islamists appeared to have been exhausted; yet they returned to the headlines with the attacks of 11 September 2001. The alleged leader of the 11

September hijackers, Mohamed Atta, was Egyptian; more important, it seems, was the role of an Egyptian cadre within the command structures of al-Qaeda and in the activist cells which prepared the 2001 attacks.

Contradictions

Since 2001 Egypt has played a key role in Washington's global security strategy. Its forces act as torturers for the US government, extracting information from detainees kidnapped across the world by agents of the CIA (see Chapter 7). In the domestic arena, this partnership legitimises and reinforces the regime's assault on civil liberties in the name of 'fighting terrorism', providing rationales for major initiatives such as the 'Anti-Terrorism Act' introduced to parliament in 2006–07 and the use of military courts to hear cases against civilians. The underlying trajectory of US policy has been to support such repression in the name of regime stability; at times, however, lip service to democratic change has been used to fend off hostility about American policy in the region.

In November 2003 President Bush delivered a speech at the National Endowment for Democracy, setting out a project for political change across the Arab world and making special reference to the government of Egypt, which, he said, 'should show the way toward democracy' in the region (Barbash 2003). In June 2005, commenting on his discussions with Mubarak, Bush insisted that free and fair elections in Egypt must be part of the process of change. This lip service to change did not continue for long, however, as Washington became alarmed at the consequences of an active reform process. American commentators close to the US administration concurred: 'If the United States pushes too far, too fast', suggested one former Bush adviser, 'the Islamists waiting in the wings will gain the upper hand' (Schenker 2006). Concerned at the electoral progress of the Muslim Brotherhood in the parliamentary elections of 2005 in Egypt, and of Hamas in Palestine, Washington had shifted from 'heady rhetoric and strong action in support of democratic transformation throughout the Middle East' to 'a cold realism that counsels warm relations with dictators in exchange for their help on counterterrorism and other strategic matters' (Schenker 2006).

Conclusion: a client state in crisis?

Three decades of economic, political and military cooperation between the USA and Egypt have left an indelible mark on the Egyptian state and on society at large. The Egyptian army relies on US weapons; US advisers shape Egypt's economy and mould the country's education system; US brands are visible everywhere as McDonald's, Coca-Cola, Pepsi and KFC repackage slices of American life for the Egyptian middle class. Today the Egyptian elite takes as a cultural reference point the values of its US counterpart: instead of the French- or Italian-styled palaces built by earlier generations, the rulers of contemporary Egypt create US-inspired communities of 'luxury fibre-optic wired villas, as shopping malls, theme parks, golf courses and polo grounds rise out of the desert' (Mitchell 1999: 28).

The mechanisms that have sustained Mubarak in power are also, however, a source of weakness for his regime. Once Britain enjoyed a similar relationship with Egypt's rulers; sixty years ago British officials and military men were deeply involved in the coercive apparatus. They worked with European financiers and entrepreneurs to shape Egypt's economy and linked Egypt to a regional strategy aimed at preserving British hegemony in the Middle East. During the 1940s and early 1950s, under the pressure of rising levels of political and social protest, destructive feedback mechanisms began to affect the Anglo-Egyptian relationship, transforming British support for the monarchy from a source of strength to a source of weakness. Repression of protests calling for the evacuation of British troops was undertaken by the Egyptian authorities – with the full support of the British government – and acted as an important radicalising influence on the national movement, prompting activists to see not only the colonial power but also the Egyptian monarchy as an obstacle to achieving their goals.

Such an outcome was by no means inevitable. Similar linkages between socio-economic grievances and political discontent shook the Sadat regime of the 1970s but did not alter his successor's commitment to alliance with the USA. Since 2003, however, the USA–Egypt relationship has become an important element in a broader crisis of the Mubarak regime. Invasion and occupation of

Iraq, and US policy vis-à-vis Palestine, have been important elements in the series of interlocking movements which developed from 2000 and which have encouraged a broad culture of protest against the Mubarak regime.

Conclusion:
What's next?

Rabab El-Mahdi & Philip Marfleet

Events in Egypt have global significance. Egypt is the pivotal state of the Arab region: its economic, political and social influence parallels that of Brazil in South America or of India in South Asia. It has the largest population in the region, the biggest productive economy and a historic status as cultural heart of the Arab world.[1] What happens in Egypt matters profoundly in the Middle East and in the wider context of the Global South, especially since a new world crisis has given urgency to debates about the impacts of neoliberalism and the effectiveness of resistance and of alternatives to the global market model.

Understanding of developments in Egypt affords comparative assessment, especially in relation to other states under the control of authoritarian regimes committed to the neoliberal agenda. How are struggles of Egyptian peasants related to those of their Chinese counterparts? How do experiences of Egyptian labour compare with those of workers in Morocco or Colombia? Are Egyptian actors for democratisation different from their peers in Brazil or Mexico during the transition of these countries to formal democracy? What is the relationship between events in Egypt and in states such as Algeria or Chile where progressive changes have been halted or reversed?

Some accounts of the long-term effect of neoliberalism suggest that it dissipates resistance and weakens collective action (Veltmeyer et al. 1998; Harvey 2005). In the case of Latin America, Eckstein asks, 'Where have all the movements gone?' She comments on 'the effects of macro economic, social and political conditions on mobilizations for change', on the disappearance of many mass movements and on the re-emergence of others in new forms (Eckstein 2001: 351). Analyses presented in this book suggest that an accelerated neoliberal agenda in Egypt has intensified contradictions, prompting diverse forms of resistance and stimulating long-dormant actors to undertake new cycles of collective contention. Rather than dissipating resistance, it has brought new urgency and new actors to the political scene.

Problems intensify

The Sadat regime of the 1970s had a claim to pioneering status: its *infitah* can be viewed as one of the first sustained attempts to move away from models of the development state which characterised post-colonial projects in the 'third' world. Thirty years later Egypt had become the World Bank's exemplar for policies of marketisation: at the same time it exhibited many of the contradictions inherent in the neoliberal project.

In 2007 US Secretary of Commerce Carlos M. Gutierrez congratulated Egyptian businessmen on their economic progress, praising record growth rates. By generalising Egypt's 'pro-growth policies', he said, 'We can expand international markets, help alleviate poverty, and boost development around the globe' (Department of Commerce 2007). Such headline accounts of growth often conceal patterns of grossly uneven development. In 2008 a Carnegie Endowment report on Egyptian economic performance was highly critical, asking 'Why don't the benefits of growth trickle down?' It suggested that shortages of bread and continuing labour protests were a stark contrast to stories of burgeoning business activity, observing: 'The gap between the rich and poor has not been reduced and unemployment levels remain stagnant' (Saif and Leone 2008). The report noted that increases in food and energy prices accounted for the bulk of inflation and had a disproportionate effect upon the poor, while the property boom had made housing unaffordable for the mass of people. It also predicted increasing difficulties, a scenario confirmed when the financial 'meltdown' of 2008 took its effect.

Growth in Egypt has been concentrated in specific sectors, notably commodities, finance, property and tourism. These seldom stimulate long-term investment or provide significant secure employment; rather, they attract speculative involvement which soon diminishes when returns begin to fall. The record growth rates of 2005 to 2007 were closely associated with 'hot' money generated in the Arab Gulf when oil prices rose to historic highs. Achcar (2009) comments that much of Egypt's 'IMF-scripted "success story"' can be attributed to investment of petrodollars promptly withdrawn when the scale of global financial collapse became apparent.

Foreign direct investment to Egypt almost halved during the first year of the world crisis (Wasser 2009).[2] Other sources of income also declined: the number of foreign visitors fell sharply and both migrant remittances and income from the Suez Canal were much diminished (Yeranian 2009; Saleh 2009). A host of analyses predicted sharp cuts in overall economic activity: one described earlier growth figures as 'a wistful memory' (Arab Finance News 2009). Having pursued the rhetoric of growth, prosperity and stability, the regime must now address both the immediate needs and the disillusion of millions of people.

Democratisation from below

Most academic analyses of contemporary Egypt have been bound by assumptions about elite politics and/or by attitudes towards political culture which emphasise 'exceptionalism'. There is a pronounced elite bias: a tendency to view continuity and change through a statist prism, with politics reduced to changing configurations among the elite and within formal institutional structures. Notwithstanding the range of issues in question – continued authoritarianism, lack of a democratic transition, change in economic policies, or rising manifestations of opposition such as political Islam – the state and the elite are the only actors of consequence (see Lust-Okar 2005; Brownlee 2007). Such approaches silence others who play a significant role, overtly or covertly, in shaping socio-economic and political agendas. Meanwhile there is a strong tendency to view events in the Middle East in the context of exceptionalism – the idea that Arab/Islamic cultures are resistant to change, especially to democratic transitions.

This book has attempted to reverse the trend, emphasising the importance of politics 'from below' and the engagement of those normally denied a role in the political field – workers, pro-democracy activists and mass-based opposition groups such the Muslim Brotherhood. It has also tried to understand Egypt as part of the Global South, affected by and exhibiting patterns that are less 'culturally specific' than part of wider trends. Contributors have highlighted a series of forms of resistance, raising questions about their relationships and outcomes. Will the question of Palestine continue to be a radicalising influence? Is there a link between the pro-democracy movement and struggles that followed? What is the impact on Islamism of other movements for change?

This book has also raised an issue that preoccupies writers on the politics of contention: the matter of structure and agency. To what extent does an authoritarian system compel or contain resistance? Was the growth of the democracy movement a function of continued repression or primarily of initiatives among the activists? Can policies of repression and co-optation contain the energies of the exploited and oppressed? Collectively the authors suggest that there is an organic relationship between structural elements and socio-political actions. A holistic approach is required – one in which the role of social agents is fully recognised. It is in this context that the chapters of Beinin, Bush, El-Mahdi, Naguib and Seif El-Dawla are of special importance, allowing us to hear something of the experiences and aspirations of those who stand outside the formal political field.

Finally, contributors raise questions about the local, the regional and the global. As Alexander makes clear, the longevity of the Arab–Israeli conflict and the occupation of Iraq have made the Egyptian state an important ally of world powers, which also play a key role in shaping domestic economic policy. Here Egypt sits within the complex of relationships in which the agendas of neoliberalism and imperialism are most clearly complementary. This generates specific challenges for the regime and for the opposition, notably the major political contender, the Muslim Brotherhood.

New actors

Egypt's president is 81 years old. There is a widespread assumption that his son, a powerful figure in the NDP, has been groomed to replace him and may be preparing to present himself in the presidential elections of 2011 – throwing down a challenge to democracy activists who have opposed dynastic succession. The regime seems disinclined to offer even mild reforms, limiting the potential for democratisation by formal procedural means. The democracy movement is weakened and the main mass opposition movement is unprepared to challenge those in power. The situation is volatile, however. New actors have emerged, disturbing the established structure of state corporatism. Industrial workers, state employees and independent media have modified the rules of the game. Each demonstrates different levels of success in terms of constituency-building, resilience and collaboration; but each has found a place on the political stage and each is likely to play a role in events to come. As we have learned from examples across the Global South, movements from below often decline and are reshaped by new pressures and social contexts, re-emerging in the form of campaigns for rights, lobbies for reform and, most importantly, from class-based initiatives which have the potential to bring sweeping change.

Notes

Introduction

1. In April 2008 Mubarak's years in power were exceeded only by Omar Bongo of Gabon (who came to power in 1967); Gadhafi of Libya (1969); Saleh of Yemen (1978); Gayoom of the Maldives (1978); Obiang of Equatorial Guinea (1979); dos Santos of Angola (1979); and Mugabe of Zimbabwe (1980).
2. See Founding Statement of the association at www.aloufok.net/article. php3?id_article=484.
3. 'Neoliberalism': a reassertion of classical/neoclassical economic principles in which restructuring of national economies takes place on the basis of supremacy of the market, deregulation and the retreat of the state from both economic and social affairs.
4. 'Top reformers in 2006/07', *Doing Business*, International Finance Corporation (World Bank), at www.doingbusiness.org/features/Reform2007.aspx.
5. See Levy 2004 on the abrupt collapse of the Argentinian economy and the implications for the mass of the population.
6. 'De-sequestration': reversal of earlier reforms under which land was taken under state control ('sequestered'). Under de-sequestration land is 'returned' to private ownership, or in effect comes under the control of new private landowners. See Chapter 3.
7. See background information on *Strategic Urban Plans for Small Cities* (UN–Habitat n.d.).
8. This term is widely used by the International Labour Organisation (ILO) to describe working lives in which wages provide incomes that barely meet official poverty levels.
9. Adel William, director of LCHR, quoted in Shahine 2008.
10. See, for example, Owen 1994; Brumberg 2002; Kassem 1999; Keinle 2001; Lust-Okar 2005; Posusney and Angrist 2005; Brownlee 2007.

Chapter 1

1. See Mansfield (1971: 223–4) on events in 1919. British soldiers were attacked and killed by protestors; British troops also shot many Egyptian demonstrators, including fourteen in the city of Tanta.
2. See Gills et al. 1999 for an account of this term in relation to political regimes in the Global South.
3. Quoted in Gazzar 2000.
4. World Bank figures quoted by El-Naggar 2005a.
5. Abaza, quoted in Hennawy 2008.
6. Fergany, quoted in *Financial Times* 2007.
7. Heikal, quoted in Baker 1978: 22.
8. Mustafa Khamis and Muhammed Hassan al-Baqari, executed in August 1952 for allegedly inciting riots at the Misr Textile Company in Kafr Al-Dawwar.
9. Report of *Al Tali'ah*, quoted in Baker 1978: 144.
10. The regime also faced problems with international financial organisations aware that bureaucratic corruption in Egypt rendered the regime increasingly vulnerable to their demands.
11. See, in Arabic, Kifaya 2006.
12. According to one of the organisation's leading members, the regime has set an example which has been copied throughout society: 'Corruption in Egypt, neglected for years, is like a cancer that has now spread to every part of the body... It is a way of life.' Quoted in Nkrumah 2006.
13. Quoted in Kassem 2004: 54.
14. Under electoral law, judges notionally have responsibility for monitoring voting and counting.
15. Quoted in Menshawy 2005.
16. Quoted in ibid.
17. See, for example, the report of the *Washington Post* on police tactics in Badawy, a small town in the Nile Delta: Williams, 2005.
18. Quoted in Hopwood 1993: 87.
19. Quoted in Baker 1978: 96.
20. Quoted in Hopwood 1993: 115.
21. Quoted in ibid.
22. After more than thirty years of legal status the New Wafd has 6 of the 454 seats in the People's Assembly, Tagammu' has 2; several well-established parties have none.
23. Comment made as part of a debate on 'Twenty years of multipartyism in Egypt' (Hussein et al. 1999: 77).
24. In 2005, as the regime suppressed demonstrations of Egypt's democracy movement, General Guide of the Brotherhood Mohamed Mahdi Akef, asserted that protest must be limited to 'symbolic' action: see Abdel-Latif 2005.
25. Haikal, quoted in Baker 1979: 189.
26. See *Forbes* list at www.zawya.com/Story.cfm/sidZAWYA20070401083826.
27. See the 'rich list' of Arab billionaires in Abdurabb 2007.

28. See Dreamland promotion at www.dreamlandegypt.com/en/about/default. aspx.
29. Quoted in *Financial Times* 2007.
30. Abdalla (1985: ch. 8) describes how two waves of national protest at university campuses broke a political 'silence' that had lasted since 1954.
31. See Ibrahim 1988.
32. Shukri, quoted in Hinnebusch 1985: 71.

Chapter 2

1. Slogans reported during street demonstrations identified the steel tycoon by name. According to Moustafa (2004), protestors chanted: 'Ahmed Ezz, living in luxury, tell us who is protecting you? Down with the monopoly of the steel mills!'
2. See , for example, the estimate of 20.2 per cent for June 2008, 'the highest in at least a decade', by Bloomberg, at www.bloomberg.com/apps/news?pid=2060III6&refer=africa&sid=ayZopaD_zIAQ.

Chapter 3

1. See also Murphy 2005.
2. *Fellahin*; sing. *fellah*: peasant or farmer. Literally tiller of the soil, from *falaha*: to split, cleave or plough. Also widely used to describe rural as opposed to urban dwellers.
3. Quoted in El-Ghonemy 1990: 228.
4. See specification at www.mwri.gov.eg/english/mubarak.asp.

Chapter 4

1. The literal translation of *al-Ittihad al-'Amm li-Niqabat 'Ummal Misr* is General Federation of Egyptian Trade Unions.
2. 'Moral economy': a term usually associated with British historian E.P. Thompson, who argued that struggles of workers and the poor should be set in the context of understandings of what is normal and appropriate in terms of incomes, living standards and the proper functionings of communities and institutions. See Thompson 1971.
3. For details, see the journalistic articles I wrote under various pseudonyms in the *Guardian* (New York): 'Sadat Throttles His Critics as Economy Worsens', 29 October 1980; 'Sadat Consolidates Power', 28 May 1980; 'Internal Opposition Shakes Sadat's Regime', 16 April 1980.
4. Hossam el-Hamalawy and I interviewed Sayyid Habib and Mohamed al-'Attar in Mahalla al-Kubra on 9 March 2007 about the December 2006 strike (see below for details) and its background. All references to information they provided come from this interview, which was a main source of our co-authored article, parts of which are adapted here. See Beinin and Hamalawy 2007.

5. According to the Central Agency for Public Mobilisation and Statistics, in 2000–01 the public and private sectors employed 209,272 workers in spinning, weaving and dyeing, and 163,241 clothing workers, compared to 457,191 spinning, weaving and dyeing workers in 1976 (CAPMAS).

6. This information is based on Mohamed al-'Attar's monthly pay slip for February 2007. Interview, 9 March 2007.

7. Interview, 19 March 2005. The interviewee requested anonymity.

8. Ibid.

9. Al Ahram Beverages increased its labour force from 3,100 to 5,500, while wages increased 200–300 per cent – a nearly unique outcome of privatisation. The San Stefano Hotel shut its doors in 1993; so it was not difficult to increase the workforce there dramatically in preparation for reopening in June 2007.

10. They included Minister of Foreign Trade and Investment Rachid Mohamed Rachid, Minister of Finance Dr Yousef Boutros-Ghali, Minister of Investment Dr Mahmoud Mohieldin, and Minister of Communication and Information Technology Dr Tarek Kamel.

11. Arab Republic of Egypt, Ministry of Trade and Industry, QIZ website www.qisegypt.gov.eg-www-english-About-about_qiz_faq.asp.

12. Land Center for Human Rights, *Isdarat al-huquq al-iqtisadiyya wa'l-ijtima'iyya* 39 (August 2005); 42 (January 2006); 53 (February 2007); 55 (July 2007) and 58 (February 2008). Egyptian Workers and Trade Union Watch reported over 580 collective actions in 2007. See Jonathan Spollen, 'Workers Take to the Streets: The Strikes of 2007', *Daily News Egypt*, 30 December 2007.

13. The agreement is recorded in a statement of al-Lajna al-Tansiqiyya li'l-Hurriyat al-Niqabiyya w'al-'Ummaliyya, the Hisham Mubarak Law Center, and Trade Union Watch, at http://arabist.net/arabawy/wp-content-uploads/2007/12/tax-strikers.pdf.

14. Interview, 9 March 2007.

15. Central Agency for Public Mobilisation and Statistics, On-Line Census of Industrial Production, 2000–01, "Adad al-mansha'at wa-'adad al-mushtaghalin hasba fi'at al-sinn wa'l-naw".

16. See report at http://arabist.net-arabawy/2007/06/14/mansoura_espana_wal-mart/.

17. See report at http://arabist.net/arabawy/2007/06/21/victory-for-the-mansoura-espana.

18. Interview with several Mansura-España workers, 9 February 2008; *Al-Badil*, 12–15 March 2009.

19. *Al-Misri al-Yawm*, 5 May 2007.

20. See the statements of 20 March and 3 April 2007 at www.ikhwanweb.com/Home.asp?zPage=Systems&System=PressR&Press=Show&Lang=E&ID=6687 and http://www.ikhwanweb.com/Home.asp?zPage=Systems&System=PressR&Press=Show&Lang=E&ID=6836.

21. Interview before a speech at the American University of Cairo, 21 November 2006.

22. Voice of America Radio, 28 September 2007.

23. See report at http://arabist.net/arabawy/2007/09/24/videos_mahalla.

24. *Al-Misry Al-Yawm*, 18 and 28 February 2008.
25. Interview with several Mahalla workers, March 20, 2009.
26. Kifaya, which showed much promise from late 2004 until mid-2005, was unable to mobilise effectively after the 2006 Lebanon War. Primarily a movement of students, intellectuals and middle-class professionals, Kifaya generally had only tenuous relations with the workers' movement. Kifaya managed to hold a demonstration in Cairo to express solidarity with the striking Mahalla workers and to protest the clampdown on freedom of the press on 27 September. But the low attendance at that event indicated a substantial disconnect between Kifaya and the workers' movement (see also Chapter 5).

Chapter 5

1. See McAdam et al. 2001.
2. The terms 'Kifaya' and 'democracy movement' are used here interchangeably. Although the former is one of multiple groups it has been the biggest and most active of these formations and has been represented in most of the latter.
3. Interview with George Ishaq, general coordinator of Kifaya, Cairo, 9 August 2006.
4. Comments reported in the Kuwaiti newspaper paper *Al-Siyasa* and the Cairo daily *Al-Ahram* and quoted in Howeidy 2005a.
5. For a report and pictures of the Shubra demonstration, see Arabawy blog: http://arabist.net/archives/2005/06/23/demo-in-shubra/.
6. Ibid.
7. Quoted in Shahine 2005.
8. According to Egyptian law, parties must be approved by a state-appointed body which has sole authority to licence public political activity. See Chapter 1.
9. Shehata (2004: 4) comments on the 'number and ideological diversity' of participants. See also Schwedler and Clark 2006.
10. Interview, Cairo, 6 July 2006.
11. The target being government attempts to 'normalise' relations with Israel by establishing trade links and collaborations.
12. Interview with A. El-Mashad, founding member of PCSI, Cairo, 27 January 2007.
13. Interview with Aida Seif El-Dawla, Cairo, 8 August 2006.
14. Interview with a member of the Kifaya steering committee of 2005, Cairo, December 2006.
15. The amendment of Article 76 was initiated by Mubarak in February 2005, with a call for multi-candidate elections for the presidency rather than the one-candidate referendum system which had been used to select the president since 1952. On 25 May 2005 there was a referendum in which voters were decide (Yes/No) on changing Article 76. Kifaya activists protested the formulation of the amendment, which was designed to sustain

presidential rule from within the NDP; they also protested the wording
of the referendum question as vague and misleading.

16. 'Protesters Attacked in Cairo', *Washington Post*, 26 May 2005.
17. Interview with A. Qandil, Kifaya spokesperson 2004–05, Cairo, August 2006.
18. Interview with activist of the Revolutionary Socialists, 31 January 2007.
19. Figures from the Egyptian Workers and Trade Union Watch report, 2007 (in Arabic). Reports are published on the Arabawy blog: http://arabist. net/arabawy. See report for April 2007 at http://arabist.net/arabawy/wp-content/uploads/2007/05/aprilreport.pdf.

Chapter 6

An earlier draft of this chapter was presented at Cairo Papers Symposium, 'Egypt: 30 years of Protest' at the American University in Cairo April 2007.

1. Also transliterated as Gamaat Islamiya, Jamaat al Islamiya, al-Jama'ah al-Islamiyah, etc.
2. For other Arab leftist versions of the same theory see Al Said 1999; Azm 1998.
3. For the pre-Nasser history of the movement see Mitchell 1969; Lia 1998.
4. Wiktorowicz (2004) provides an excellent collection of studies applying SMT to Islamism in a number of Arab countries. See particularly his theoretical introduction.
5. Foucault (1994) famously labelled the Iranian Revolution as the first post-modern revolution.
6. There were limits however, even during the mid-1970s, to the tactical alliance between the new Muslim Brotherhood and the Sadat regime. The regime refused the legalisation of the Brotherhood and its leader, Omar al-Tilmissani, refused to be appointed by Sadat as a member of the Shura council (an offer later accepted from Mubarak by Rifaat Al Said, the 'leftist opposition' leader of the National Progressive Unionist Party).
7. Beinin, along with many commentators on the secular left, sees the growth of Islamist student groups and their dislodging of leftist dominance as a result of 'a combination of intimidation, physical force, and provision of services', like cheap photocopies of textbooks and transportation for women who wore the hijab (Beinin 2005: 119). This account underestimates both the failure of the left to stand up to the challenge posed by the growing Islamic movement and the real ability of the latter to become a radical alternative to thousands of students.
8. For more details, see Azzam 2006.
9. See http://arabist.net/archives/2006/08/05/the-muslim-brothers-support-for-lebanon.
10. See the heated debate on this issue between Abdel Meneim Abu Al-Futuh and Mohamed Mursi (both leading members of the Brotherhood) in the pages of *Dustur*, October 2007.

Chapter 7

1. Testimony of the victim to staff of the El Nadim Center.
2. Testimonies to the El Nadim Center.
3. See, for example, articles in the *Financial Times*, 13 January 2007; *Time* magazine, 23 January 2007; and *Le Figaro*, 10 October 2007.
4. See United Nations General Assembly resolution A/RES/39/46, 10 December 1984.
5. See Founding Statement at www.aloufok.net/article.php3?id_article= 484.
6. Former CIA official Robert Baer, in Stephen Grey, 'America's Gulag', *New Statesman*, 17 May 2004, quoted in Human Rights Watch 2005.
7. Quoted Calabresi 2007.
8. Statement by Egyptian activists: 'Egypt is Wearing Black in Mourning', at www.beirut.indymedia.org/ar/2005/06/2710.shtml.
9. 'Mubarak has forgotten a word: "Torture"', Bahgat 2005.
10. Statement issued in Cairo on 15 August 2007 and signed by: Arab Network for Human Rights Information, Association for Freedom of Thought and Expression, Association for Human Rights Legal Aid, Bariq Association against Violence against Women, Centre for Human Rights Studies and Legal Information, Centre for Socialist Studies, Centre for the Rights of the Egyptian Child, Committee of Liberties at the Press Syndicate, Egyptian Association Against Torture, El Awn Egyptian Association for Human Rights, El Fagr Centre for Human Rights, El Horeyya Centre for Political Rights and Support of Democracy, Hisham Mubarak Law Centre, Land Center for Human Rights, Mosawat Association – Port Said, Nadim Centre for the Rehabilitation of Victims of Violence, Shumu'u Centre for the Rights of the Disabled, Sons of the Land Center for Human Rights.
11. Ibid.

Chapter 8

1. Economic aid, in the form of grants from Washington's Economic Support Fund (ESF) grant averaged $818 million per year between 1991 and 1997. In 1998 the US agreed a ten-year phased reduction in economic aid to Egypt, which brought the ESF grant down to $450 million by the end of 2007 (Sharp 2007: 27–9).
2. Other states have recently increased their share of trade, notably China, which is expected to overtake the USA as Egypt's biggest trading partner by 2012 (Sharp 2007: 21).
3. The original terms of the agreement set the proportion of Israeli imports at 11.7 per cent. The timing of the agreement was an indication of pressure on the Egyptian government to soften the impact on Egyptian manufacturers of removal of quotas for textiles and clothing exports with the expiration of the international Multi-Fibre Agreement in 2005 (Sharp 2007). A World Bank report assessing Egypt's performance a year after the end of the MFA suggested that the QIZ scheme was largely responsible for an 8 per

cent rise in Egyptian textiles and clothing exports to the USA in 2005–6 (World Bank 2006b: 21).

4. The text of the agreement can be found in Usher 1997: 120.

Conclusion

1. Egyptian GDP in 2008 at purchasing power parity (PPP) was estimated at $452.5 billion. The only state in the Arab region with a larger GDP was Saudi Arabia at $600.4 billion, of which almost half came from oil revenues. In terms of broader productive capacities, Egypt remains the economic giant of the region. See *CIA World Factbook* for current figures: www.cia.gov/library/publications/the-world-factbook/index.html.

2. One estimate suggests that FDI had reduced by 44 per cent, as foreign investors quickly retreated. See Wasser 2009.

References

Abaza, M. (2001) 'Shopping Malls, Consumer Culture and the Reshaping of Public Space in Egypt', *Theory, Culture and Society*, vol. 18, no. 5.

Abdalla, A. (1985) *The Student Movement and National Politics in Egypt*, Al Saqi, London.

Abdel-Aal, M. (2003) *Agrarian Relations in Transition: The Impact of the Change in Tenancy Law on Agricultural Work and Production in Qena and Aswan*, final report mimeo, Social Research Centre, Cairo.

Abdel-Fadil, M. (1975) *Development, Income Distribution and Social Change in Rural Egypt 1952–1970: A Study in the Political Economy of Agrarian Transition*, Cambridge University Press, Cambridge.

Abdel-Fadil, M. (1980) *The Political Economy of Nasserism*, Cambridge University Press, Cambridge.

Abdel-Kader, T. (1988) 'State, Capital and Workers' Protests in Egypt', M.A. thesis, American University in Cairo

Abdel-Latif, O. (2005) 'The Shape of Things to Come', *Al-Ahram Weekly*, 31 March – 6 April.

Abdel-Malik, A. (1968) *Egypt, Military, Society: The Army Regime, the Left, and Social Change under Nasser*, Vintage Books, New York.

Abdel-Rahman, M. (2009) "With the Islamists? – Sometimes. With the State? – Never!' Co-operation between the Left and Islamists in Egypt', *British Journal For Middle East Studies*, vol. 36, no. 1.

Abdoun, S. (2008) 'Ministry of Interior Suspends 280 Policemen', *Daily News* (Cairo), 29 December .

Abdurabb, K. (2007) 'Saudis Lead List of Arab Billionaires', *Arab News*, 2 April.

Abrahamian, E. (1992) 'Khomeini: Fundamentalist or Populist?', *New Left Review* 186, March/April.

Achcar, G. (2004) 'Marxists and Religion Yesterday and Today', *International Viewpoint*, www.internationalviewpoint.org.

Achcar, G. (2006) 'Eleven Theses on the Resurgence of Islamic Fundamentalism', *International Viewpoint*, www.internationalviewpoint.org.

Achcar, G. (2009) 'Egypt's Recent Growth: An "Emerging Success Story"?', *Development Viewpoint* 22, February.

Adams, R.H., Jr (2000) 'Evaluating the Process of Development in Egypt 1980–97', *International Journal of Middle East Studies*, vol. 32, no. 2.

Ahmed, A.A.M. (1995) *Al-Harakat al-Islamia fi Misr wa Qadiet al-Tahawul al-Dimuqrati* (The Islamist Movements in Egypt and Democratic Transition), Markaz al-Ahram, Cairo.

Akef, M. (2007) 'Weekly Message', October, www.ikhwanonline.com.

Al-Ahram (2006) *Economic Strategic Report 2006*, Al-Ahram Press, Cairo.

Al-Ahram (2008) *Economic Strategic Report 2008*, Al-Ahram Press, Cairo.

Al-Bishri, T. (1983) *Al-haraka al-siyasiyya fi misr 1945–1952* (The Political Movement in Egypt 1945–1952), Dar al-shuruq, Cairo.

Al-Erian, E.(2003) Commentary, www.ikhwanonline.com, 4 May.

Al-Erian, E. (2004) Interview, www.ikhwanonline.com, 8 June.

Al-Gamal, S. (2007) 'Contradiction et Mangue de Transparence', www.hebdo. ahram.org.eg/arab/ahra/2007/5/16/evep2.htm.

Al-Ghazali, A.H. (1990) 'Sanat Al-Taghyir wa Iradat Al-Bina' (The Year of Change and the Will to Build), *Al-Nur*, January.

Al-Said, R. (1999) *Hassan al-Banna: Mata, Kayfa wa Limadha* (Hassan al-Banna: When, How and Why?), Cairo, Al-Hay'a Al-Misria Al-Ammah lil Kitab).

Alexander, A. (2007) *Leadership in the National Movements of Egypt and Iraq: 1945–1963*, Ph.D. thesis, University of Exeter.

AmCham (American Chamber of Commerce in Egypt) (2004a) 'The Egyptian Economy: Progress and Prospects', www.amcham.org.eg/operation/Events/Events04/agm.asp.

AmCham (American Chamber of Commerce in Egypt) (2004b) *The Textile and Clothing Industry in Egypt*, AmCham, Cairo.

AmCham (American Chamber of Commerce in Egypt) (2006) 'Egypt and the US: Investing in Partnership, Report of the Door Knock Mission to Washington, D.C. – Qualifying Industrial Zones in Egypt', www.amcham.org. eg-BSAC-ustrade-pdffiles-QIZBrochure06.pdf.

Amin, S. (2001) 'Political Islam', *Covert Action Quarterly* 71.

Amnesty International (2002) 'Egypt: No Protection – Systematic Torture Continues', www.amnesty.org/en/library/info/MDE12/031/2002.

Amnesty International (2007a) 'Egypt: Continuing Crackdown on Muslim Brotherhood', http://asiapacific.amnesty.org/library/Index/ENGMDE120282007? open&of=ENG-EGY.

Amnesty International (2007b) 'Egypt: Systematic Abuses in the Name of Security', www.amnesty.org.uk/uploads/documents/doc_17663.pdf.

Amnesty International (2008a) *Amnesty International Report 2008*, http://thereport. amnesty.org/eng/Regions/Middle-East-and-North-Africa/Egypt.

Amnesty International (2008b) 'Emergency Court Rulings on Mahalla Protests Entrench Abuses', Amnesty International, London.

ANHRI (Arabic Network for Human Rights Information) (2007) 'Clarification Needed from the Assistant to the Minister of Interior – 5/1,000 What?', http://anhri.net/en/focus/2007/pro120.shtml.

Ansari, H. (1987) *Egypt: The Stalled Society*, American University in Cairo Press, Cairo.

Arab Finance News (2009) 'Beltone cuts Egypt growth projections', https://www.arabfinance.com/News/newsdetails.aspx?Id=132108.

Ashour, O. (2008) 'De-Radicalization of Jihad? The Impact of Egyptian Islamist Revisionists on Al-Qaeda', *Perspectives on Terrorism*, vol. 2, no. 5.

Awlad al Ard Human Rights Organisation (2007a) 'Report on Dandeet and Survey of Tenants and Near-Landless', mimeo, Cairo.

Awlad al Ard Human Rights Organisation (2007b) 'Violence in Egypt's Countryside', mimeo, Cairo.

Ayubi, N. (1991) *The State and Public Policies in Egypt since Sadat*, Ithaca, Reading.

Azimi, N. (2005) 'Egypt's Youth Have Had Enough', *Open Democracy*, www.opendemocracy.net/democracy-protest/enough_2794.jsp.

Azm, S.J. (1998) *Al-almania wa al-mujtama al-madani* (Secularism and Civil Society), Centre for Legal and Human Rights Information, Cairo.

Azzam, M. (2006) 'Islamism Revisited', *International Affairs*, vol. 82, no. 6.

Bahgat, H. (2005) 'Mubarak Has Forgotten a Word: "Torture"', *Daily Star* (Cairo), www.eipr.org/en/commetry/dailystar/dailystar_comm_1.htm.

Baker, R. (1978) *Egypt's Uncertain Revolution Under Nasser and Sadat*, Harvard University Press, Cambridge MA.

Bakry, R. (2008) 'Public Outcry over Talk of Subsidy Reform', *Business Monthly* (American Chamber of Commerce in Egypt), January.

Bandy, J., and S. Smith (2005) *Coalitions across Borders: Transnational Protest and the Neoliberal Order*, Rowman & Littlefield, Lanham MD.

Barbash, F. (2003) 'Bush: Iraq Part of "Global Democratic Revolution"', *Washington Post*, 6 November.

Bayat, A. (1993) 'Populism, Liberalization and Popular Participation: Industrial Democracy in Egypt', *Economic and Industrial Democracy* 14.

Bayat, A. (2005) 'Islamism and Social Movement Theory', *Third World Quarterly*, vol. 26, no. 6.

BBC (2006) 'Violence at Cairo Trial Protest', http://news.bbc.co.uk/1/hi/world/middle_east/4760487.stm.

BBC (2008a) 'Egypt Cracks Down on Gaza Protest', http://news.bbc.co.uk/2/hi/middle_east/7205403.stm.

BBC (2008b) 'Gaza Conditions "at Forty Year Low"', http://news.bbc.co.uk/1/hi/world/middle_east/7280026.stm.

BBC (2008c) 'Jibes Highlight Bush–Mubarak Rift', http://news.bbc.co.uk/1/hi/world/middle_east/7410669.stm.

Beinin, J. (1985) 'The Cold Peace', *Middle East Report*, no. 129.

Beinin, J. (1993) 'Will the Real Egyptian Working Class Please Stand Up?', in Z. Lockman, ed., *Workers and Working Classes in the Middle East: Struggles, Histories, Historiographies*, State University of New York Press, Albany NY.

Beinin, J. (2001) *Workers and Peasants in the Modern Middle East*, Cambridge University Press, Cambridge.

Beinin, J. (2005a) 'Political Islam and the New Global Economy: The Political Economy of an Egyptian Social Movement', *New Centennial Review*, vol. 5, no. 1.

Beinin, J. (2005b) 'Popular Social Movements and the Future of Egyptian Politics', *Middle East Report Online*, www.merip.org/mero/mero031005.html.

Beinin, J. (2007) 'Neo-liberal Structural Adjustment, Political Demobilization, and Neo-Authoritarianism in Egypt', paper delivered at 'The Dynamics of Change in the Arab World: Globalisation and the Re-Structuring of State Power', International Affairs Institute, Rome, 16–18 July.

Beinin, J. (2008) 'Underbelly of Egypt's Neo-liberal Agenda', *Middle East Report Online*, www.merip.org/mero/mero040508.html.

Beinin, J., and H. Hamalawy (2007) 'Strikes in Egypt Spread from Center of Gravity', *Middle East Report*, May, www.merip.org/mero/mero050907.html.

Beinin, J., and Z. Lockman (1987) *Workers on the Nile*, Princeton University Press, Princeton.

Biersteker, T. (2000) 'Globalization as a Mode of Thinking in Major Institutional Actors', in N. Woods, ed., *The Political Economy of Globalization*, Macmillan, London.

Black, I. (2007) 'A Country in Crisis as Fearful Government Cracks Down on Islamist Opposition', *Guardian*, 17 July.

Bromley, S., and R. Bush (1994) 'Adjustment in Egypt? The Political Economy of Reform', *Review of African Political Economy* 60.

Brownlee, J. (2002) 'The Decline of Pluralism in Mubarak's Egypt', *Journal of Democracy*, vol. 13, no. 4.

Brownlee, J. (2007) *Authoritarianism in an Age of Democratization*, Cambridge University Press, Cambridge.

Brumberg, D. (2002) 'Democratization in the Arab World? The Trap of Liberalized Autocracy', *Journal of Democracy*, vol. 13, no. 4.

Burgat, F., and W. Dowell (1993) *The Islamic Movement in North Africa*, University of Texas Press, Austin.

Burns, J. (2000) 'The Rich: Echoes of a Pharaonic Past', *Financial Times,* http://specials.ft.com/ln/ftsurveys/country/sc2b06.htm.

Bush, R. (1999) *Economic Crisis and the Politics of Reform in Egypt*, Westview Press, Boulder CO.

Bush, R. (2004) 'Poverty and Neo-liberal Bias in the Middle East and North Africa', *Development and Change*, vol. 35, no. 4.

Bush, R. (2007) 'Mubarak's Legacy for Egypt's Rural Poor: Returning Land to the Landlords', in A. Haroon Akram-Lodhi, S.M. Borras Jr and C. Kay, eds, *Land, Poverty and Livelihoods in an Era of Globalization*, Routledge, London and New York.

Bush, R., ed. (2002) *Counter-Revolution in Egypt's Countryside: Land and Farmers in the Era of Economic Reform*, Zed Books, London.

Butter, D. (1992) 'Egypt', *Middle East Economic Digest*, Special Report, June.

Calabresi, M. (2007) 'Bush's Dangerous Torture(d) Stance', *Time*, 5 October.

CAPMAS (Central Agency for Public Mobilisation and Statistics Online Census of Industrial Production) (2001) 'Adad al-mansha'at wa-'adad al-mushtaghalin hasba fi'at al-sinn wa'l-naw'.

Carr S. (2008a) 'Increase Minimum Wages to Match Price Increase', *Daily News* (Cairo), 29 February.

Carr, S. (2008b) 'Egypt Ranks 115 in Global Corruption Index', *Daily News* (Cairo), 23 September.

Carr, S. (2008c) 'Activists Lash Out against State Security over Prisoners of Conscience', *Daily News* (Cairo), 5 December.

Carr, S. (2008d) 'Observers Ask Why Demonstrations Fall Flat without the Muslim Brotherhood', *Daily News* (Cairo), 30 December.

Central Bank of Egypt (2008) *Monthly Statistical Bulletin*, January.

Chalcraft, J. (2004) *The Striking Cabbies of Cairo and Other Stories: Crafts and Guilds in Egypt, 1863–1914*, State University of New York Press, Albany NY.

Chomsky, N. (1999) *The Fateful Triangle: The United States, Israel and the Palestinians*, Pluto, London.

Cooper, M. (1982) *The Transformation of Egypt*, Johns Hopkins University Press, Baltimore MD.

Craig, G. (2008) 'Worth More Than Gold', *Business Monthly* (American Chamber of Commerce in Egypt), September.

Cuno, K.M. (1992) *The Pasha's Peasants: Land, Society and Economy in Lower Egypt, 1740–1858*, American University in Cairo Press, Cairo.

Darwish, Y. (2008) 'New Capmas Study Shows Unemployment Slightly Decreasing', *Daily News* (Cairo), 18 September.

Denis, E. (2006) 'Cairo as Neo-liberal Capital? From Walled City to Gated Communities', in D. Singerman and P. Amar, eds, *Cairo Cosmopolitan*, American University in Cairo Press, Cairo.

Dethier, J.J., and K. Funk (1987) 'The Language of Food: PL 480 in Egypt', *Middle East Report* 145, March–April.

Diehl, J. (2005) 'Mubarak Outdoes Himself: Election Fraud Backfires', *Washington Post*, 5 December.

Diehl, J. (2007) 'Forsaking the Egyptian Free Press', *Washington Post*, 24 September.

EAAT (Egyptian Association Against Torture) (2003) statement, www.aloufok. net/article.php3?id_article=484.

EAAT (Egyptian Association Against Torture) (2005) *Torture Record in the Year of Reform: A Review*, www.amannet.org/reportnadim1.html.

Eckstein, S. (2001) 'Where Have All the Movements Gone? Latin American Social Movements at the New Millennium', in S. Eckstein, ed., *Power and Popular Protest: Latin American Social Movements*, University of California Press, Berkeley.

The Economist (2005) 'The New Pharaohs', 10 March.

The Economist (2007) 'A Summer of Discontents: Egypt's Political and Economic Problems', 9 August.

The Economist (2008) 'Egypt: Will the Dam Burst?', 11 September.

Egypt State Information Service (2005) 'Demand on Telecom Egypt's Share Stimulates the Egyptian Stock Exchange', www.sis.gov.eg/En/Economy/ New/0509000000000000003.htm.

Egyptian Central Bank (2008) *Statistics Newsletter*, Cairo.

El-Bassiouni, M., and O. Saeed (2007) 'Strike Flags in the Egyptian Sky: A New

Labor Movement in 2007' (in Arabic), Center for Socialist Studies, Cairo.

El-Din, G. (2000) 'A Future for Fruits', *Al-Ahram Weekly*, 13–19 January.

El-Din, G. (2003) 'MPs Strike Back', *Al-Ahram Weekly*, 8–14 May.

El-Din, G. (2006) 'Nazif Upbeat on Economy', *Al-Ahram Weekly*, 21–27 December.

El-Din, G. (2008a) 'Sifting through the Embers', *Al-Ahram Weekly*, 21–27 August.

El-Din, G. (2008b) 'Still an Emergency', *Al-Ahram Weekly*, 29 May–4 June.

El-Gawhary, K. (1997) "Nothing More to Lose': Landowners, Tenants, and Economic Liberalization in Egypt', *Middle East Report* 204.

El-Ghonemy, M.R. (1990) *The Political Economy of Rural Poverty: The Case for Land Reform*, Routledge, London and New York.

El-Ghonemy, M.R. (1993) 'Food Security and Rural Development in North Africa', *Middle Eastern Studies*, vol. 29, no. 3.

El-Ghonemy, M.R. (1999) 'Recent Changes in Agrarian Reform and Rural Development Strategies in the Near East', *Land Reform*, vols. 1 and 2.

El-Madany, S. (2008) '20 Egyptian Cement Executives Found Guilty of Price-Fixing', *Daily News* (Cairo), 25 August.

El Nadim Center for Psychological Management and Rehabilitation of Victims of Violence (2006) *Torture in Egypt: Facts and Testimonies* (in Arabic), El Nadim Center, Cairo.

El Nadim Center for Psychological Management and Rehabilitation of Victims of Violence (2007) *Torture in Egypt: Facts and Testimonies 2003–2006* (in Arabic), El Nadim Center, Cairo.

El-Naggar, A. (2005a) 'Massaging the Figures', *Al-Ahram Weekly*, 8–14 December.

El-Naggar, A. (2005b) *Economic Decay in the Mubarak Era* (in Arabic), Dar Merit, Cairo.

El-Nahas (2009) M. 'Pointless Parties', *Al-Ahram Weekly*, 1–6 January.

El-Shafei, O. (1995) 'Workers, Trade Unions and the State in Egypt, 1984–1989', *Cairo Papers in Social Science*, vol. 18, no. 2, American University in Cairo Press, Cairo.

Elyan, T., and A. Salah-Ahmed (2008) 'Steel Tycoon Responds to Accusations of Monopoly', *Daily News* (Cairo), 25 June.

Falk, R. (2002) 'Interpreting the Interaction of Global Markets and Human Rights', in A. Brysk (ed.) *Globalization and Human Rights*, University of California Press, Berkeley.

Falk, R. (2003) *The Great War on Terror*, Arris Books, Moreton-in-Marsh.

Farag, F. (2003) 'Green Desert – At What Cost?', *Al-Ahram Weekly*, 23–29 January.

Faris, M.A., and M.H. Khan (eds) (1993) *Sustainable Agriculture in Egypt*, Lynne Rienner, Boulder CO and London.

Fathi, Y. (2005) 'When the Strangers Came to Town', *Al-Ahram Weekly*, 21–27 April.

Fergany, N. (2002) 'Poverty and Unemployment in Rural Egypt', in R. Bush, ed., *Counter Revolution in the Egyptian Countryside*, Zed Books, London.

FIDH (Fédération Internationale des Droits de l'Homme) (2005) 'State of Emergency', www.fidh.org/spip.php?article2264.

Financial Times (1999) *Financial Times Survey: Country Briefs, Egypt*, 18 June.

Financial Times (2007) *Special Report on Egypt*, 10 December.

Fisk, R. (1990) *Pity the Nation: Lebanon at War*, Deutsch, London.

Fisk, R. (2009) 'The Rotten State of Egypt is Too Powerless and Corrupt to Act', *Independent*, 1 January.

Fletcher, L.B. (ed.) (1996) *Egypt's Agriculture in a Reform Era*, Iowa State University Press, Ames.

Follath, F., et al. (2006) 'America's Shame: Torture in the Name of Freedom', *Der Spiegel*, 20 February, www.spiegel.de/international/spiegel/0,1518,401899,00. html.

Foucault, M. (1994) 'Reponse de Michel Foucault à une Lectrice Iranienne', in *Dits et Écrits*, vol. 3, Gallimard, Paris.

Gazzar, B. (2000) 'The Ballot and the Bullet', *Cairo Times*, 2–8 November.

Gills, B., J. Rocamora and R. Wilson (1999) *Low Intensity Democracy: Political Power in the New World Order*, Pluto, London.

Gordon, J. (1992) *Nasser's Blessed Movement*, Oxford University Press, Oxford.

Government of Egypt (1990) *Agricultural Census 1990*, Ministry of Agriculture, Cairo.

Government of Egypt (2000) *Agricultural Census 2000*, Ministry of Agriculture, Cairo.

Government of Egypt (2005a) *Bulletin of Foreign Trade 2005*, Ministry of Agriculture and Land Reclamation, Cairo.

Government of Egypt (2005b) 'Support to NEPAD–CAADP Implementation TCP/EGY/2905(I) (NEPAD Ref 05/29 E)', *National Medium Term Investment Programme*, vol. 1, December 2005, Government of Egypt, Cairo.

Habeeb, W (2002) 'US–Egypt Aid Negotiations in the 1980s and 1990s', in I. Zartman and J. Rubin, eds, *Power and Negotiation*, University of Michigan Press: Ann Arbor.

Halawi, J. (2005) 'Terror to Torture', *Al-Ahram Weekly*, 27 January–2 February.

Hamood, S. (2006) *African Transit Migration through Libya to Europe: The Human Cost*, Forced Migration and Refugee Studies, American University in Cairo.

Hamzawy, A. (2005) 'Opposition in Egypt Performance in the Presidential Election and Prospects for the Parliamentary Elections', *Carnegie Endowment Policy Outlook*, 1–6 October.

Handoussa, H. (1991) *Employment and Structural Adjustment: Egypt in the 1990s*, American University in Cairo Press, Cairo.

Harel, A., and A. Issacharoff (2006) 'Israeli Defence Official: Fatah Arms Transfer Bolsters Forces of Peace', *Ha'aretz*, 28 December.

Harel, A., and A. Issacharoff (2007) 'Fatah to Israel: Let Us Get Arms to Fight Hamas', *Ha'aretz*, 7 June.

Harvey, D. (2005) *A Brief History of Neoliberalism*, Oxford University Press, Oxford.

Hennawy, N. (2008) '(Window) Shop – Till You Drop', *Egypt Today*, vol. 29, no. 2, February.

Henry, C., and R. Springborg (2001) *Globalization and the Politics of Development in the Middle East*, Cambridge University Press, Cambridge.

Hinnebusch, R. (1985) *Egyptian Politics under Sadat*, Cambridge University Press, Cambridge.

Hinnebusch, R. (1990) 'The Formation of the Contemporary Egyptian State from Nasser and Sadat to Mubarak', in I.M. Oweiss, ed., *The Political Economy of Egypt*, Center for Contemporary Arab Studies, Georgetown University, Washington DC.

Hirst, D., and I. Beeson (1981) *Sadat*, Faber & Faber, London.

Hopwood, D. (1993) *Egypt, Politics and Society 1945–1990*, Routledge, London.

Howeidy, A. (2005a) 'The Taboos Are Broken', *Al-Ahram Weekly*, 19–25 May.

Howeidy, A (2005b) 'Prison is Like Death', *Al-Ahram Weekly*, 20–26 October.

Howeidy, A. (2006) 'Democracy's Backlash', *Al-Ahram Weekly*, 9–15 March.

Human Rights Watch (1992) *Behind Closed Doors*, New York.

Human Rights Watch (2001) 'Egypt: Human Rights Background', www.hrw. org/backgrounder/mena/egypt-bck-1001.htm.

Human Rights Watch (2003) 'Egypt's Emergency without End', New York.

Human Rights Watch (2004) 'Egypt's Torture Epidemic', www.hrw.org/english/ docs/2004/02/25/egypt7658.htm.

Human Rights Watch (2005a) *Egypt: Attacks by Security Forces in Sarando*, New York.

Human Rights Watch (2005b) *From Plebiscite to Contest: Egypt's Presidential Election* New York.

Human Rights Watch (2005c) 'Black Hole: The Fate of Islamists Rendered to Egypt', www.hrw.org/reports/2005/egypt0505/1.htm#_Toc102563427.

Human Rights Watch (2005d) 'Egypt: Investigate Police for Sudanese Deaths', www. hrw.org/en/news/2005/12/29/egypt-investigate-police-sudanese-deaths.

Human Rights Watch (2005e) 'Is There a Human Rights Double Standard? US Policy Toward Saudi Arabia, Iran, Uzbekistan, and Pakistan', www.hrw. org/english/docs/2007/06/14/usint16481.htm.

Human Rights Watch (2006a) 'Egypt: Investigate Election Fraud, Not Judges' www. hrw.org/en/news/2006/04/24/egypt-investigate-election-fraud-not-judges.

Human Rights Watch (2006b) 'Egypt: Police Assault Demonstrators, Journalists' www.hrw.org/en/news/2006/05/11/egypt-police-assault-demonstrators-journalists.

Human Rights Watch (2007a) 'Egypt: Bus Driver Raped by Police Faces New Risk of Torture', www.hrw.org/english/docs/2007/01/13/egypt15060.htm.

Human Rights Watch (2007b) 'Egypt: Extending State of Emergency Violates Rights: Repressive Law Renewed in Place of Promised Reform',www.hrw. org/english/docs/2008/05/28/egypt18951_txt.htm.

Human Rights Watch (2008a) 'Egypt: Jailing 800 Activists Casts Doubt on Elections', 28 May, www.hrw.org/en/news/2008/03/29/ egypt-jailing-800-activists -casts-doubt-elections.

Human Rights Watch (2008b) 'Egypt: Investigate Beating of "Facebook" Activist: Authorities Use Intimidation, Violence to Suppress Online Advocacy', http://hrw.org/english/docs/2008/05/10/egypt8800_txt.htm.

Human Rights Watch (2008c) 'Egypt: Extending State of Emergency Violates Rights', statement at: www.hrw.org/english/docs/2008/05/28/egypt18951. htm.

Human Rights Watch (2008d) 'Egypt: New Indictments in HIV Crackdown', www.hrw.org/english/docs/2008/03/11/egypt18257.htm.

Hussein, A., R. al-Said and M. al-Sayyid (1999) 'Twenty Years of Multipartyism in Egypt', in M. Kennedy, ed., *Twenty Years of Development in Egypt*, Cairo Papers in Social Science, vol. 21, no. 3, American University in Cairo Press, Cairo.

Ibrahim, A. (1999) 'Keeping the Military Balance Skewed', *Al-Ahram Weekly*, 5–11 August.

Ibrahim, A. (2007) 'Star Loses Magnitude', *Al-Ahram Weekly*, 8–14 November.

Ibrahim, S. (1988) 'Domestic Developments in Egypt', in W. Quandt, ed., *The Middle East Ten Years after Camp David*, Brookings Institution, Washington DC.

Ibrahim, S., and H. Löfgren (1996) 'Successful Adjustment and Declining Governance? The Case of Egypt', in L. Frischak and I. Atiyas, eds, *Governance, Leadership, and Communication*, World Bank, Washington DC.

ICRT (International Rehabilitation Council for Torture Victims) (2005) 'Appeal to Egypt: End Torture', www.irct.org/Default.aspx?ID=159&M=News&PID=12000&NewsID=195.

ILO (International Labour Organisation) (2009) *Global Employment Trends January 2009*, ILO, Geneva.

IMF (International Monetary Fund) (1990) *International Financial Statistics Yearbook*, IMF, Washington DC.

IMF (International Monetary Fund) (2007) *International Financial Statistics Yearbook*, IMF, Washington DC.

IRIN (2006) 'Egypt: Corruption Hampering Development, Says Opposition Report', *Humanitarian News and Analysis*, UN Office for the Coordination of Humanitarian Affairs, www.irinnews.org/report.aspx?reportid=27105.

IRIN (2007) 'Plight of Palestinian Refugees Worsening in Most Parts of the Middle East', *IRIN News*, www.irinnews.org/Report.aspx?ReportId=72841.

Johnstone, C. (2008) 'In Egypt, Long Queues for Bread that's Almost Free', Reuters, 6 April.

Kassem, M. (1999) *In the Guise of Democracy*, Ithaca Press, London.

Kassem, M. (2004) *Egyptian Politics: The Dynamics of Authoritarian Rule*, Lynne Rienner, Boulder CO.

Kepel, G. (1985) *Muslim Extremism in Egypt: The Prophet and the Pharaoh*, University of California Press, Berkeley.

Kershner, I., and T. El-Khodary (2007) 'Violence Escalates in Gaza between Hamas and Fatah', *International Herald Tribune*, 11 June.

Kienle, E. (2001) *A Grand Delusion: Democracy and Economic Reform in Egypt*, I.B. Tauris, London.

Kifaya (2004) Statement, www.harakamasria.org; in English, www.harakamasria.org/node/2944.

Kifaya (2006) *Corruption in Egypt: A Black Cloud That Never Passes* (in Arabic), http://harakamasria.org/files/tqrer.pdf.

King, R. (1977) *Land Reform: A World Survey*, G. Bell, London.

Knight, L. (2007) *Post-Privatizaton Impact Assessment: Final Report – A Review of 17 Companies*, USAID, Cairo.

Kuran, T. (1989) 'Sparks and Prairie Fires: A Theory of Unanticipated Political Revolution', *Public Choice*, vol. 61, no. 1.

Lahiff, E., S.M. Borras Jr and C. Kay (2007) 'Market-Led Agrarian Reform: Policies, Performance and Prospects', *Third World Quarterly*, vol. 28, no. 8.

Land Center for Human Rights (Markaz el Ard) (2002) 'Farmer Struggles Against Law 96 of 1992', in R. Bush, ed., *Counter Revolution in Egypt's Countryside*, Zed Books, London.

Langhor, V. (2000) 'Cracks in Egypt's Electoral Engineering', *Middle East Report Online*, 7 November, www.merip.org/mero/mero110700.html.

Leila, R. (2007) 'Up in Flames', *Al-Ahram Weekly*, 29 March 29–4 April.

Leila, R. (2008) 'No Flow: Potable Water is Becoming a Scarce Commodity', *Al-Ahram Weekly*, 11–17 September.

Levinson, C. (2005) 'Egypt's Growing Blogger Community Pushes Limit of Dissent', *Christian Science Monitor*, 24 August.

Levy, M.L. (2004) *We Are Millions: Neo-liberalism and New Forms of Political Activism in Argentina*, Latin America Bureau, London.

Lia, B. (1998) *The Society of Muslim Brothers in Egypt: The Rise of an Islamic Mass Movement 1928–1942*, University of Chicago Press, Chicago.

Lust-Okar, E. (2005) *Structuring Conflict in the Arab World: Incumbents, Opponents and Institutions*, Cambridge University Press, Cambridge.

Mabrouk, M., and R. El-Bakry (2004) 'Gold Rush', *Egypt Today*, September.

Mansfield, P. (1969) *Nasser's Egypt*, Penguin, Harmondsworth.

Mansfield, P. (1971) *The British in Egypt*, Weidenfeld & Nicolson, London.

Marsot, A. (1985) *A Short History of Modern Egypt*, Cambridge University Press, Cambridge.

Mayer, J. (2005) 'Outsourcing Torture: The Secret History of America's "Extraordinary Rendition" Program', *New Yorker*, 14 February.

McAdam, D., S. Tarrow and C. Tilly (2001) *Dynamics of Contention*, Cambridge University Press, Cambridge.

Mekay, E. (2004) 'Abu Ghraib Tactics Inspire Torture in Neighbor Egypt', *Inter Press*, 22 June, www.ipsnews.het.interna.asp?idnews=24311.

Menshawy, M. (2005) 'Tough Week for Election Press', *Al-Ahram Weekly*, 17–23 November.

Meyer, D., and N. Whittier (1994) 'Social Movement Spill Over', *Social Problems*, vol. 41, no. 2.

Ministry of Finance (2007) *Customs Tariff According to the Amendments of the Harmonized System 2007*, Presidential Decree 39/2007. Cairo, Dar al-Kutub Wal Watha'eq.

Mitchell, R. (1969) *The Society of the Muslim Brothers*, Oxford University Press, Oxford.

Mitchell, T. (1991) 'America's Egypt: Discourse of the Development Industry', *Middle East Report* 169, March–April.

Mitchell, T. (1995) 'The Object of Development: America's Egypt', in J. Crush, ed., *Power of Development*, Routledge, London.

Mitchell, T. (1999) 'Dreamland: The Neo-liberalism of Your Desires', *Middle East Report* 210, Spring.

Mitchell, T. (2002) *Rule of Experts: Egypt, Techno-Politics, Modernity*, University of California Press, Berkeley.

Momani, B. (2005) *IMF–Egyptian Debt Negotiations*, Cairo Papers in Social Science, vol. 26, no. 3, American University in Cairo Press: Cairo.

Moussa, N. (2006) 'Private Sector's Share of GDP Rises Sharply', *Daily News* (Cairo), 20 July.

Moustafa, T. (2004) 'Protests Hint at New Chapter in Egyptian Politics', *Middle East Report Online*, 9 April, www.merip.org/mero/mero040904.html.

Mubarak, H. (1995) *Al-Irhabiyun Qadimun: Dirasa Muqarana bayn Mawqif al-Ikhwan al-Muslimin wa Jamaat al-Jihad min Qadiet al-Unf (1928–1994)*, Al Mahrusa, Cairo.

Murphy, D. (1995) 'The Object of Development: America's Egypt', in J. Crush, ed., *Power of Development*, Routledge, London.

Murphy, D. (1998) 'The Market's Place', in N. Hopkins and K. Westergaard, eds, *Directions of Change in Rural Egypt*, American University in Cairo Press, Cairo.

Murphy, D. (2005) 'Discontent Flaring in Rural Egypt', *Christian Science Monitor*, 6 May.

Murphy, D. (2007) 'As Egypt Cracks Down, Charges of Wide Abuse', *Christian Science Monitor*, 10 October.

Muslim Brotherhood (2007) *Al-Birnamij al-Intikhabi lil Ikhwan al-Muslimin* (Election Programme of the Muslim Brotherhood), Muslim Brotherhood, Cairo.

Nafie, R. (2007) 'Dealing with the Bread Queue Crisis', *Daily News* (Cairo), 25 December.

Nassar, S. (1993) 'The Economic Impact of Reform Programs in the Agricultural Sector in Egypt', mimeo, Ministry of Agriculture, Livestock and Fishery Wealth and Land Reclamation, Economic Affairs Sector, Cairo.

Nkrumah, G. (2006) 'Viva Corruption', *Al-Ahram Weekly*, 13–16 July.

Nkrumah, G. (2008) 'Challenges and Opportunities', *Al-Ahram Weekly*, 15–21 May.

Owen, R. (1994) 'Socio-economic Change and Political Mobilization: The Case of Egypt', in G. Salamé, ed., *Democracy without Democrats*, I.B. Tauris, London.

PACE (Papers of the Annual Conference of Egyptian Economists) (1978) *The Egyptian Economy in 25 years: 1952–1977*, Egyptian General Agency for Books, Cairo.

Popham, P., and J. Taylor (2007) 'The War on Terror: Inside the Dark World of Rendition', *Independent*, 8 June.

Posusney M.P. (1993) 'Collective Action and Workers' Consciousness in Contemporary Egypt', in Z. Lockman, ed., *Workers and Working Classes in the Middle East: Struggles, Histories, Historiographies*, State University of New York Press, Albany.

Posusney, M.P. (2003) 'Globalisation and Labor Protection in Oil-Poor Arab Countries: Racing to the Bottom?', paper presented at 'The Jordanian Economy in a Changing Environment', University of Jordan, Amman, 22–23 July.

Posusney, M.P., and M. Angrist (2005) *Authoritarianism in the Middle East: Regimes and Resistance*, Lynne Riener, Boulder CO.

Powell, C.L. (2001) 'Remarks with Egyptian Minister of Foreign Affairs Ahmed Maher', US State Department, 26 September, www.state.gov/secretary/former/powell/remarks/2001/5066.htm.

Pratt, N. (1998) *The Legacy of the Corporatist State: Explaining Workers' Responses to Economic Liberalisation in Egypt*, University of Durham Centre for Middle Eastern and Islamic Studies, Middle East Paper no. 60, November.

Pratt, N. (2007) *Democracy and Authoritarianism in the Arab World*, Lynne Rienner, Boulder CO.

Radwan, S., and E. Lee (1986) *Agrarian Change in Egypt: Anatomy of Rural Poverty*, Croom Helm, London.

Rady, F. (2005a) 'Esco Ordeal Ends', *Al-Ahram Weekly*, 2–8 June 2–8.

Rady, F. (2005b) 'Twice as Dead', *Al-Ahram Weekly*, 7–13 July.

Rashed, D. (2005) 'To Salvage a City', *Al-Ahram Weekly*, 3–15 January.

Rashed, D. (2006) 'The Art of Mismanagement: Too Many Disasters and Not a Single Plan', *Al-Ahram Weekly*, 31 August–6 September.

Regular, A. (2004) 'Palestinian Factions Attack Gaza Plan', *Ha'aretz*, 9 June.

Richards, A. (1991) 'The Political Economy of Dilatory Reform: Egypt in the 1980s', *World Development*, vol. 19, no. 12, December.

Rose, D. (2008) 'The Gaza Bombshell', *Vanity Fair*, April.

Roy, S. (2007) *Failing Peace: Gaza and the Palestinian–Israeli Conflict*, Pluto, London.

Rural Migration News (2002) 'California Commodities', www.migration.ucdavis. edu/rmd/commodities/php?ir=607_0_5_0.

Saad, R. (1999) 'State, Landlord, Parliament and Peasant: The Story of the 1992 Tenancy Law in Egypt', in A. Bowman and E. Rogan, eds, *Agriculture in Egypt from Pharaonic to Modern Times*, Proceedings of the British Academy vol. 96, Oxford University Press, Oxford.

Saad, R. (2000) 'Agricultural Politics in Contemporary Egypt: The Tenancy Crisis', *Cairo Papers in Social Science*, vol. 22, no. 4.

Saad, R. (2002) 'Egyptian Politics and the Tenancy Law', in R. Bush, ed., *Counter-revolution in the Egyptian Countryside*, Zed Books, London.

Sadiki, L. (2000) 'Popular Uprisings and Arab Democratization', *International Journal of Middle East Studies*, vol. 32, no. 1.

Sadowski, Y. (1991) *Political Vegetables? Businessman and Bureaucrat in the Development of Egyptian Agriculture*, Brookings Institution, Washington DC.

Safieddine, H. (2005) 'Ballot Boxes Burned', *Al-Ahram Weekly*, 24–30 November.

Said, E. (1994) *The Politics of Dispossession: The Struggle for Palestinian Self-determination 1969–94*, Chatto & Windus, London.

Saif, I., and A. Leone (2008) 'Why Don't the Benefits of Growth Trickle Down?', *Arab Reform Bulletin*, May.

Saiid, S. (1989) *Man Yamluk Misr* (Who Owns Egypt), Dar El-Thaqafa, Cairo.

Saleh, H. (2007) 'Egypt Bloggers Fear State Curbs', BBC News, 22 February, http://news.bbc.co.uk/1/hi/world/middle_east/6386613.stm.

Saleh, H. (2009) 'Tourism in Egypt Suffers in Crisis', *Financial Times*, 18 February.

Saleh, Y. (2008) 'Egypt Accused of Being Part of Israeli Conspiracy', *Daily News* (Cairo), 29 December.

Samaan, M. (2008) 'New Martyrs: Crisis Escalates with 15 "Bread Queue" Deaths', *Daily News Egypt*, 17 March.

Sami, S. (2005) 'Extreme Measures', *Al-Ahram Weekly*, 24–30 November.

Sayyid, S. (2003) *A Fundamental Fear: Eurocentrism and the Emergence of Islamism*, Zed Books, London.

Schemm, P. (2003) 'Egypt Struggles to Control Anti-War Protests', *Middle East Report*, 31 March.

Schenker, D. (2006) 'Policy Review', *New Republic Online*, 21 June, www.washingtoninstitute.org/templateC06.php?CID=940.

Schwedler, J., and J. Clark (2006) 'Islamist–Leftist Cooperation in the Arab World', *ISIM Review* 18, Autumn.

Selim, T.H. (2006) 'Monopoly: The Case of Egyptian Steel', *Journal of Business Case Studies*, vol. 2, no. 3.

Shahine, A. (2008) 'Egyptian Urban Inflation Rises to 23.6 per cent', *Daily News* (Cairo), 10 September.

Shahine, G. (2005) 'Summer of Discontent', *Al-Ahram Weekly*, 18–25 May.

Shahine, G. (2008) 'Dying to Live', *Al-Ahram Weekly*, 21–27 February.

Shalabi, A. (2008) 'Ezz Accused of Steel Monopoly and Irregularities in Dekheila Deal', *Al Masri Al Yom*, 24 May.

Sharp, J. (2004) *Egypt–US Relations*, Brief for Congress, Congressional Research Service, Washington DC.

Sharp, J. (2007) *Egypt: Background and US Relations*, Report for Congress (RL 33003), Congressional Research Service, Washington DC.

Sharp, J. (2008) *The Egypt–Gaza Border and its Effect on Israeli–Egyptian Relations*, Report for Congress (RL 34346), Congressional Research Service, Washington DC.

Shehata, S. (2003) 'In the Basha's House', *International Journal of Middle East Studies*, vol. 35, no. 1, February.

Shehata, S. (2004) 'Opposition Politics in Egypt: A Fleeting Moment of Opportunity', *Arab Reform Bulletin*, vol. 2, no. 9.

Shukrallah, H. (2006) 'Min al-Bayt Ila Mawqi' al-'Amal: Dirasa 'an Zuruf al-'Amala al-Nisa'iyya Fi Misr', *Tiba* 8, December.

Springborg, R. (1989) *Mubarak's Egypt: Fragmentation of a Political Order*, Westview, Boulder CO.

Springborg, R. (1990) 'Rolling Back Egypt's Agrarian Reform', *Middle East Report*, vol. 20, no. 5, September–October.

Stack, L. (2007) 'Mansoura Workers Attack Factory Sale, Sit-in Reaches Day 20', *Daily Star*, 11 May.

Stack, L., and M. Mazen (2007) 'Striking Mahalla Workers Demand Government Fulfill Broken Promises', *Daily News Egypt*, 27 September.

State Information Service (2006) (Cairo), www.sis.gov.eg/En/Politics/.

Stephens, R. (1971) *Nasser*, Penguin, Harmonsworth.

Tarrow, S. (1998) *Power in Movement: Social Movements and Contentious Politics*, Cambridge University Press, Cambridge.

Thompson, E.P. (1971) 'The Moral Economy of the English Crowd in the 18th Century', *Past & Present* 50: 76–136.

Tingay, C. (2004) 'Agrarian Transformation in Egypt: Conflict Dynamics and the Politics of Power from a Micro Perspective', Ph.D. thesis, Freie Universität Berlin.

Trade Arabia (2007) 'Alwaleed Backs Toshka', 12 March, www.tradearabia.com/news/newprint.asp?Article=120294&Sn=AGRI.

UNDP (United Nations Development Programme) (2008) *Egypt: Human Development Report*, UNDP, Cairo.

UN–Habitat (n.d.) *Strategic Urban Plans for Small Cities*, www.unhabitat.org/content.asp?cid=4402&catid=192&typeid=13&submenuId=0.

United Nations (2006) 'Assessment of the Future Humanitarian Risks in the Occupied Palestinian Territory', 11 April, www.reliefweb.int/library/documents/2006/ocha-opt-11apr.pdf.

UNOCHA (UN Office for Co-ordination of Humanitarian Affairs) (2006) 'Egypt: Poverty Rampant in Rural Areas, Says New Report', *IRIN News*, 13 February.

USAID (1992a) *Country Program Strategy FY 1992–1996: Egypt*, USAID, Cairo.

USAID (1992b) *Country Program Strategy FY 1992–1996: Agriculture*, USAID, Cairo.

USAID (1998a) 'USAID/Egypt Agriculture', www.info.usaid.gov/eg/econ.htm.

USAID (1998b) 'USAID/Egypt Economic Growth Overview', www.info.usaid.gov/eg/econ-ovr.htm.

USAID (1999) *Agriculture: Vision for 2003*, RDI policy brief, MALR/USAID Agricultural Policy Reform Programme, Cairo.

USAID (2000) 'Egypt: Congressional Presentation', http://usaid.gov/pubs//cp2000/ane/egypt/html.

USAID (2008) 'Working Together for Egypt: A Prosperous Country, a Prosperous People', http://egypt.usaid.gov/.

USAID and Government of Egypt (1995) 'The Egyptian Agricultural Policy Reforms: An Overview', presented at Agricultural Policy Conference 'Taking Stock, Eight Years of Egyptian Agricultural Policy Reforms', 26–28 March.

US Census Bureau (2008) 'Trade in Goods (Imports, Exports and Trade Balance) with Egypt', *Foreign Trade Statistics*, www.census.gov/foreign-trade/balance/c7290.html.

US Congress (2006) *Congressional Budget Justification for FY 2006, Foreign Operations*, www.nsaid.gov/policy/budget/cbj2006/glossary.html.

US Department of Commerce (2007) (United States of America, Department of Commerce), 'Secretary of Commerce Carlos M. Gutierrez – American Chamber of Commerce in Egypt Washington, D.C.', statement issued 15 March., at www.commerce.gov/NewsRoom/SecretarySpeeches/PROD01_002827.

US Government (2007) *Summary and Highlights, International Affairs Function 150: Fiscal Year 2008 Budget Request*, www.state.gov/documents/organization/80151.pdf.

US State Department (2008) 'Background Note on Egypt', www.state.gov/r/pa/ei/bgn/5309.htm.

Usher, G. (1997) *Palestine in Crisis*, Pluto Press, London.

Utvik, B. (2006) *Islamist Economics in Egypt*, Lynne Rienner, Boulder CO.

Veltmeyer, H., J. Petras and S. Vieux (1997) *Neoliberalism and Class Conflict in Latin America: A Comparative Perspective on the Political Economy of Structural Adjustment*, Macmillan, London.

Wahish, N. (2006) 'The Three Musketeers', *Al-Ahram Weekly*, 5–11 January.

Wasser, L. (2009) 'FDO Inflows Expected to Fall, Say Analysts', *Daily News* (Cairo), 22 February.

Waterbury, J. (1983) *The Egypt of Nasser and Sadat*, Princeton University Press, Princeton NJ.

Waterbury, J. (1985) 'The Soft State and the Open Door: Egypt's Experience with Economic Liberalisation 1974–84', *Comparative Politics*, vol. 18, no. 1.

White House (2005a) 'President Sworn-In to Second Term', Inauguration 2005, 20 January, www.whitehouse.gov/news/releases/2005/01/20050120–1.html.

White House (2005b) 'President and South African President Mbeki Discuss Bilateral Relations', 1 June, www.whitehouse.gov/news/releases/2005/06/20050601.html.

Wickham, C.R. (2002) *Mobilizing Islam: Religion, Activism, and Political Change in Egypt*, Columbia University Press, New York.

Wiktorowicz, Q. (2004) *Islamic Activism: A Social Movement Theory Approach*, Indiana University Press, Bloomington.

Williams, D. (2005a) 'Protesters Attacked in Cairo', *Washington Post*, 26 May.

Williams, D. (2005b) 'In Egypt's Countryside, Farmers' Anger Seen as "Silent Time Bomb"', *Washington Post*, 17 July.

Williams, D. (2005c) 'Police Attack Voters During Last Day of Egypt Election', *Washington Post*, 8 December.

World Bank (1990) *World Development Report*, Washington DC.

World Bank (1995) *World Development Report*, Washington DC.

World Bank (2001a) *Arab Republic of Egypt Toward Agricultural Competitiveness in the 21st Century: An Agricultural Export Oriented Strategy*, report no. 23405–EGT, 21 December, Washington DC.

World Bank (2001b) *Egypt Social and Structural Review*, report no.22397–EGT, 20 June, Washington DC.

World Bank (2002) *SDF Beyond 2002*, Washington DC.

World Bank (2004) *World Development Indicators*, Washington DC.

World Bank (2005) *World Development Report 2005*, Washington DC.

World Bank (2006a) *World Development Indicators*, Washington DC.

World Bank (2006b) *Morocco, Tunisia, Egypt and Jordan after the end of the Multi-Fiber Agreement*, Social and Economic Development Sector Unit, Middle East and North Africa Region, Washington DC.

World Bank (2007a) *World Bank Country Brief: Egypt*, October, http://siteresources. worldbank.org/integypt/resources/egypt-eng2007am.pdf.

World Bank (2007b) *World Development Indicators*, Washington DC.

World Bank (2008) *World Bank Worldwide Governance Indicators*, http://info.world-bank.org/governance/wgi.

Yadav, V. (2007) 'The Political Economy of the Egyptian–Israeli QIZ Trade Agreement', *Middle East Review of International Affairs*, vol. 11, no. 1.

Yapp, M.E. (1996) *The Near East Since the First World War: A History to 1995*, Long-man, London and New York.

Yeranian, E. (2009) 'Egyptian Economists Worry about Falling Suez Canal Revenues', *VoA News*, 23 February.

Zaalouk, M. (1989) *Power, Class and Foreign Capital in Egypt: The Rise of the New Bourgeoisie*, Zed Books, London.

Zaki, R. (1985) *Research in Egypt's Foreign Debts* (in Arabic), Madbouli Press, Cairo.

Zubaida, S. (1993) *Islam, the People and the State: Essays on Political Ideas and Movements in the Middle East*, I.B. Tauris, London.

All websites accessed 2 April 2009.

Contributors

Anne Alexander is an ESRC postdoctoral researcher at the School of Oriental and African Studies, London University. She has written widely on Arab affairs, notably on recent developments in Egypt and Iraq, and is the author of *Nasser: His Life and Times* (2005) and *The Rise of Political Islam* (2007).

Joel Beinin is Donald J. McLachlan Professor of History and Professor of Middle East History at Stanford University, and formerly director of Middle East Studies at the American University in Cairo. He is the author of numerous works on Egyptian, Palestinian and Israeli history, notably (with Zachary Lockman) *Workers on the Nile: Nationalism, Communism, Islam, and the Egyptian Working Class, 1882–1954* (1987).

Ray Bush is Professor of African Studies and Development Politics, University of Leeds, and former visiting professor at the Social Research Centre, the American University in Cairo. He has published very widely on globalisation, agrarian reform in Africa and the Middle East, and land tenure in Egypt. He is editor of *Counter-Revolution in Egypt's Countryside: Land and Farmers in the Era of Economic Reform* (2002).

Rabab El-Mahdi is Assistant Professor of Political Science at the American University in Cairo. She has worked at McGill University in Canada and for the Canadian International Development Agency. She has written on movements of protest in Egypt, on the Egyptian women's movement, and on modern Egyptian history.

Ahmed El-Sayed El-Naggar is an economic analyst at the Ahram Center for Political and Strategic Studies, Cairo. He is the author of numerous analyses of Egyptian economic affairs, and is editor-in-chief of the *Arab Strategic Report*. His *Political and Economic Consequences of the Iraq Catastrophe* was published in Arabic in 2003.

Philip Marfleet is Reader in Refugee Studies at the University of East London. He formerly worked at the American University in Cairo. He has published widely on migration and refugees, globalisation and anti-globalisation, social and political movements in the Middle East, and religious activism. He is the author of *Refugees in a Global Era* (2006).

Sameh Naguib teaches Development Studies at the American University in Cairo. He has worked as a journalist and academic and has written widely on Egyptian affairs, including for *Al-Ahram Weekly* and *Christian Science Monitor*. An analysis of Islamism in Egypt, *The Muslim Brotherhood: A Critical Perspective*, was published in Arabic in 2005.

Aida Seif El-Dawla is Professor of Psychiatry at Ain Shams University, Cairo. She is a founder member of the El-Nadim Center for Psychological Management and Rehabilitation of Victims of Violence, and of the Egyptian Network for Human Rights. She has written numerous reports on human rights, torture and other forms of abuse. In 2003 she received the Human Rights Watch Award.

Index